TERRY
VENABLES'
FOOTBALL
HEROES

*To my wife Yvette, my family and friends –
thank you for your support.*

First published in Great Britain in 2001 by

Virgin Books

Thames Wharf Studios, Rainville Road

London, W6 9HA

A catalogue record for this book is available from the British Library.

This edition produced for
The Book People Ltd,
Hall Wood Avenue, Haydock,
St Helens WA11 9UL

ISBN 1 85227 037 3

Designed by Balley Design Associates

Printed and bound in Italy

TERRY VENABLES' FOOTBALL HEROES

TERRY VENABLES

WITH JANE NOTTAGE & ALEX MONTGOMERY

TED SMART

'I think Terry is one of the best
coaches in the world right now.
The game is all about strategy
and he was one of the first
coaches to really work on the
technical side of a match when
he was in charge at Barcelona.
I have great admiration for him.'
PELE

Contents

Introduction

There hasn't been a day in the last 30 years of my career as a coach when I haven't been asked to give my opinion on the game. I have rarely said no. I have always been one to ask questions of my tutors, good or bad, from when I was a youngster just stepping into the game and dreaming of being a professional to the present day. So now, as a teacher (and that's what a coach is) I am happy to be asked by those who feel I may be able to supply the answers. If you are prepared to ask questions, it cuts down the learning time; it makes you more knowledgeable quicker.

When Virgin approached me to see if I might like to nominate my 'Football Heroes', I was delighted to say yes. I realised that it would give me the opportunity to highlight the people who answered so many of my questions and who made an impact on my career in football and my life in general.

It also allowed me the added luxury of immersing myself in wonderful memories about great occasions I have been part of as player or coach or simply an observer. They have all contributed to a game constantly evolving, always demanding more from those involved, always capable of surprising you with its gracefulness and beauty at the highest level. It can be a beautiful game.

Each and every one of the 40 Heroes I have named has taught me something of value – they have opened my mind to so many factors: tactics, strategy and technique; how to treat others; how to regard fitness; how to be alert; how to see the possibilities football offers (off and on the field); how to realise you have to be fulfilled away from the game; the value of friendship.

It wasn't just about choosing between Alfredo di Stefano and Ferenc Puskas either. They were both great performers, but at an important moment it was di Stefano who enlightened me as a young man, pierced the darkness, with a pass, a movement, stealth. It stuck in a young brain desperate for knowledge, to understand, to try and emulate.

Nor is it just about world-rated players. It's about many individuals – nowhere near as celebrated – who stopped long enough in my life to invest me with a desire to improve, to take on board good habits as second nature (to respect good, honest people, for example), to listen and to learn.

In England during my time there has been a handful of innovative coaches and I am pleased to say I have worked with them all and learned from them all. Dick Foss was the first who tried to make youngsters look more deeply at the game – deeper than three circuits of the track and then home. Dave Sexton took that a stage further and taught me to study the game from every angle, including that of the strategy coaches of American Football, the grid-iron variety. Don Howe was an excellent all round coach, so highly regarded by the players he worked with and coaches like myself. Malcolm Allison was inventive, a coach who would gamble with new ideas, sometimes totally without caution, and could have been one of the original 40 Heroes. They know my opinion of them and how much the game acknowledges their contribution to English football. They were men ahead of their time.

There may be an argument about naming the world's greatest footballer, but there is none about the contenders – di Stefano, Pele, Cruyff. They were musts on my list alongside Bobby Moore, and George Best and Bobby Charlton and John Charles and Johnny Haynes and the long since departed Duncan Edwards and a particular Scottish hero of mine, Denis Law. Many great coaches, like Ron Greenwood and Bob Paisley, didn't make the list but that is not to underestimate their unique contributions to our game during the sixties, seventies and into the eighties.

As for players, Kevin Beattie possessed outstanding qualities that I admired from afar. I met Kevin for the first time at a dinner in London recently when I had the chance to tell him of my admiration. Paul McGrath I tried but failed to sign on more than one occasion for Tottenham, so highly did I consider his ability. There are perhaps startling omissions, no Ruud Gullit for instance nor Frank Rijkaard, but I have concentrated on those whose path has crossed with mine, however fleetingly. Please accept I didn't sit down and ask, 'Who are the world's greatest players?' or, 'Who are the greatest managers and coaches?' The Heroes in this book, I repeat, are my personal choices.

I love coaching. I get a buzz from working and planning, and of course winning, that I can't get from anything else I have done. What my experience tells me is this: if we don't find a solution to the problem of producing first-class coaches – and that is the province of the Football Association and presumably their technical director Howard Wilkinson – then there will be no time in the future when the FA will feel that there is an Englishman good enough to coach England. One of the great ironies of the current situation is that we have employed a Swede in Sven-Goran Eriksson at the precise moment when the best group of young players for years is emerging. I am not against Sven because he is not English. I am against the appointment because the FA seems to think there is no-one else capable of doing the job. And, no, I'm not thinking of myself – that's history.

The senior coaches in football have the most important of roles. So much depends on them and we must find ways to make them better teachers. The FA has put together courses that produce the initial groundwork, the organisation required by those determined to take on the job of coach. But after having their proficiency tested, there must be another step forward for these coaches; they need to learn how to be 'result providers'. Unfortunately, what these courses have never done is show coaches how to win matches – the very thing they need to know.

The player production cycle – if that's what we can call it – begins with the youth team. A great example in the modern game is at Manchester United where the kids are found, nurtured and prepared for senior football. From that very early age they are taught the game. They then have to prove they can sustain the highest level of commitment and the players, if good enough and strong enough, will go on and be asked to attain results against better teams and in far tougher company. The man responsible for ensuring they do that is Sir Alex Ferguson.

Winning is the lifeblood of football clubs – that is an undeniable fact. But if we consider the ideal it would be to win and win with grace and style and verve; to win without the sort of fear that inhibits talent; to win beautifully and in a way that dissolves the opposition, renders it harmless. Brazil did just that in 1970, Holland four years later. They are the two examples I can use to illustrate my point. In 1970 the Brazilians beat Italy with a team we have to consider the greatest assembled and with football as perfect as we can imagine. The Italians were good but Brazil were at the pinnacle. To coach that group of players, to arrange that team would be the ideal. Not only did they play to the highest standard, but also they knew they had to work to win. They were endowed with every quality a coach could ask for.

Four years later I watched the Dutch team of Rinus Michels and was in awe of their brilliance, but a little confused. Here was a team that were not only European but nearly as good as the best produced by Brazil, yet they had a population not much bigger than that of London to draw their players from. Year after year the Dutch have produced world-class performers, been acclaimed European Champions and involved in World Cup finals. They have maintained an incredibly high standard for decades now. They lost in 1974 to a German team managed by Helmut Schoen, but a team that lumbered in comparison in the final. Holland were superb, West Germany (as they then were), stubborn and in a win-no-friends mood. I accept the need to win, I accept the delight the result would have brought to the German nation. But if push came to shove I am not sure I wouldn't rather have been Michels that day, playing the way Holland did, and lose, than Schoen.

Holland were inspirational throughout the tournament. The neutrals wanted them to win because the football they produced was what the game is about; it was exactly how you want to see it played. It was a strange feeling for a professional who isn't supposed to care how you win – so long as you win. The role of a coach has to include proving that dreams are possible. You must strive to give the people what they want because if you don't and lose then you are giving them nothing. What do they want? To feel they have seen something quite special.

Coaching and leadership are soul mates. They don't always come together, but they certainly should. The coach must know his subject, be able to convince his players he knows it, and be able to transfer his knowledge to them. He must show tolerance and understanding through his coaching, then the great determination needed to make it work. It is not enough to say, 'The coaching session is finished' and leave it at that. If the players come back to you and ask for clarification you don't say, 'I've already told you.' You talk to them again. You keep on talking until every one of them understands. It's no good if your three smartest players understand and the rest don't. Every single one of them must comprehend. The coach must always say to himself, 'I have told them, but have I *taught* them?'

There must be freedom for players, freedom to express themselves. But they must realise that there has to be discipline, though I am not talking about army-style discipline. Freedom combined with good organisation, a team plan they understand clearly so they know exactly what role they have to play. If you can show them something that will make them better players, then they will follow you.

They certainly must respect you. They won't do anything just because you have told them to. They have inner hopes, big dreams, and you must make these come alive, touch something from within, the reason why they became entranced with the game. You must show them optimism and keep pessimism to yourself. They must have pride: that is vital. If your players are frightened they will not enjoy what they are doing. It is not enough simply to tell them; as a coach you must lead without fear but with caution.

When I first started in the game, it wasn't unusual for clubs to do nothing more than try and keep

players fit, pick a team and hope they were better than the opposition. Around that ABOVE: **With Pele.** time there was a view to ban players working with the ball for three days before a match, the thinking behind this being that would make them more desperate to use it on match day. It's hard to believe but true. From that the talk went to tactics, then more set-pieces. Thanks to coaches like Dave Sexton (he wasn't the only one but the one I knew as a leader), we were coming up with new ideas. We were looking to introduce the element of surprise in matches.

At Queens Park Rangers in the early eighties I implemented the offside tactic. It was criticised but it got us into Europe, so you could also argue it was successful. We were looking at the opposition in an effort to exploit their weaknesses against our strengths. Teams weren't just rigidly set out and the system strictly adhered to from start to finish. There were changes to be made at half-time, refinements.

Now, at the beginning of the new millennium, coaches make tactical re-adjustments whenever necessary. The modern coach must be capable of doing that. Claudio Ranieri at Chelsea is one who changes his tactics during the game, though he understands that you don't change for the sake of it – the alterations must be for a reason. The modern coach must be part of the game, every moment of it, when in the past more often than not a match would finish as it started, with no attempt at addressing problems as they became evident.

At Middlesbrough I had what I called a 'whole and parts' system. It is how we trained. If there's a problem with the right side, change it; don't change the whole team. If a car doesn't start a mechanic will look for the fault and replace it. That's what we did at Middlesbrough. We trained for all possibilities. If I thought we might need one or two plans of action, then we worked on both so in the game our strategy could be changed if needed on command.

When people question the importance of tactics, it really frustrates me. If you are Manchester United or Arsenal then your attitude may be 'you prepare for us'. They will have a different approach before they meet each other but at Middlesbrough, for example, you must study as for a battle and prepare your players accordingly. It isn't easy, but it can be uplifting for the players especially when you are winning: practice, as I have always believed, makes permanent. When you are a youth you rejoice in practice: in the

first team it is business. All training must be geared to the next match. It's not necessary for the players to enjoy it; they are working to win. Training means making yourself better for the team. The day you say your game can't improve is the day you may as well just give up altogether. Experience, we are told, is wasted on the old; it's true that the young have no experience but an excess of the enthusiasm the old no longer have. But an old head with experience that retains his enthusiasm like Bobby Robson is pure gold to any club. Returning to football with Middlesbrough re-invigorated me – the best thing I could have done. I loved it. From my experience, the enthusiasm is simply waiting to be called on and comes back quicker than you think.

These days coaches have to be better because they are dealing with players who will expect more by way of explanation from them. They require much more than circuit training. The coach has to be alive to so many things. It helps when you can depend on people around you as I was able to do at Barcelona with Alan Harris, a former Chelsea team-mate. We were able to live the dream we had as young players.

The coach has to identify the stars who bring with them outstanding ability but maybe also arrive with a severe sting in the tail. Some players simply cannot be depended on; they come and go without explanation, on a whim. We even hear of the foreign players who don't want to play as often as they are asked to. But these players are still the illusion the game must have. I remember Luis Nunez, the main man at Barcelona, telling me the standard of football from Spanish players was high but to go and buy three foreign names, the bigger the better, the more expensive the better. 'Give the fans an illusion,' he would tell me. If the team was doing less than well it offered the supporters something to dream about, something to look forward to. Nunez was basically buying time but the illusion had to materialise – the players brought in could not disappoint. It would be no good if the illusion disappeared into thin air. The character of world stars will have to be scrutinised more closely than before, a process now essential to cut down the chance of clubs being seriously let down by prima donnas.

Having said that, there's no game without the players. It's they that provide the entertainment for the paying supporters. So isn't it laughable when directors worth hundreds of millions of pounds complain about the high salaries of players? It's another odd aspect of the modern game.

But still the coach's role is crucial. He is the man who pulls the strings together, the man whose expertise you bank on to provide results. Everyone demands success and only the coach can satisfy the demand by getting the best out of players. It is in his power. If football is the 'new religion', then the stadium is the 'new church'; it is where so many fans throughout the world share a common passion.

The businessmen and the corporate institutions desperate to become involved with football are beginning to recognise the importance of the coach. This is confirmed by the salaries being paid to coaches in return for the success they bring the club. A number of those businessmen still don't realise they cannot have both the power and the glory. Nunez possessed the wisdom to realise he couldn't have both. He had the power and the deep satisfaction of knowing he was the man who led from the very top. At Manchester United it's been Martin Edwards with the power and Sir Alex Ferguson the glory. That's the way it is. The coach will have the glory that comes from success – or the sack. Brian Clough once said, 'Directors are at their worst when you're winning. When you're losing they don't know what to do. But when you win they will be at the front of the picture with the cup.' He was right. Club directors claim to be tough, expert businessmen but so many of them are unsupportive of the men they appoint. They are the type who will tell you behind closed doors in hushed tones about a coach or manager they've sacked. 'Of course you realise what really happened …' – a nudge and a wink.

Power and glory! In my opinion, Howard Wilkinson wanted both with England. He had power at the FA and that allowed him to take over the running of the Under-21 national side. It was hardly a successful additional undertaking, in my view, and recently he had the responsibility taken away. Why did he cross the line and go for glory?

The way I see it, Kate Hoey, who was sacked as Minister of Sport, displayed her own lack of knowledge as a glory seeker when she complained that one of the reasons for her demise was the obsession we have with football. Didn't it click with her that it's politicians who are obsessed? It's not about what government can do for football but what football can do for government. She fell out with her own people because she wanted their power as well as the glory of the job she had. An error of judgement, as far as I'm concerned.

Football is the biggest single marketable item on the planet – after cola and burgers. Politicians want to be seen as part of it, feeding the beast. All sports are important but football is a phenomenon. There was a time when supporters and shareholders were the same people – no longer, or very rarely. These days the directors demand financial results while the priority of the supporter is, as always, to be entertained by watching a team they can be proud of. If you make £10 million and are relegated, are you a success?

There are reasons to fear for the future of the game. Despite the staggering prosperity of, and interest in, football worldwide, no-one with the power knows the best way forward and they refuse to ask those who do know what it should be. A strategy must be found to protect the good and eradicate the crazier elements that have crept in and threaten the game's stability.

I am an optimist, so I fervently believe football is too important to too many people, too much part of their lives, for them to allow it to wither on the vine. Each year we will gather more memories and find new heroes – just like the ones who inspired me.

Personal Heroes

Gordon Williams

Broadening My Horizons

I FIRST MET GORDON WHEN I WAS AT CHELSEA. AGENTS WERE JUST BEGINNING TO COME INTO THE GAME AT THIS POINT SO ONLY VERY FEW PEOPLE HAD REPRESENTATION. GORDON WAS WORKING FOR ONE OF THESE AGENCIES. HE USED TO WRITE ARTICLES FOR BOOKS FOR SOME OF THE PLAYERS SUCH AS BOBBY MOORE AND DENIS LAW AND HE WOULD GET PAID SOMETHING LIKE £25 OR £50 PER ARTICLE.

He used to tell me, 'I feel like I'm a proper writer. I shouldn't be doing this.' He penned these articles between writing his own books but he would say to the players, 'Look, why don't you do this yourself and keep all the money.' Invariably they told him that they would prefer him to do it.

Gordon said the same thing to me. I was writing an article called 'The jokes the fans don't hear' about the funny things that happen on the pitch. Gordon said, 'Why don't you write it on your own, Terry.' I said, 'Why?' Gordon replied, 'You get to keep all the money.' 'What a good idea,' I said. 'So I can cut you out just like that?' Right from early on we had that kind of banter going on between us.

So when Gordon said I had to go out and record some experiences in life, we both knew what he meant.

I bought myself a Brother pale blue typewriter and learned how to type with two fingers because that is how Gordon did it and he was so quick. Then I went to typing college which was great, particularly because there were so many girls. Somewhere there is a photo of me surrounded by 20 girls. I thought I had struck gold! I went on a touch-typing course and managed to get up to about 25 words a minute. I guess I could have had a career as a secretary had anybody wanted to take me on! The touch-typing did not last, though, and I went back to typing with two fingers – it was so much easier.

We wrote the article on 'The jokes the fans don't hear' and we received £25 each. With the money I bought a typewriter and of course, under Gordon's own instructions, I proceeded to try and cut him out … in the nicest possible way. Next I wrote a story about Sammy Small, a Londoner who went to live in Newcastle, where a group of villains got their hooks into him and he ended up a criminal. Gordon liked the piece. My prose wasn't great but I had a good ear for dialogue and the rhythm of dialogue. Gordon chuckled while reading it for the first time. I asked him what he was laughing at, the grammatical errors? He told me it wasn't that; he thought it was good. I said, 'I can't write. I'm just making it up really . I'm not educated. It's the people from Oxford and Cambridge who write.' He replied, 'No. The people from Oxford and Cambridge are the editors and sub-editors. They spend all their time in the office so they have no experience of life. They've got nothing to write about.' This was all done in a joking manner between friends, good friends. So when Gordon said I had to go out and record some experiences in life, we both knew what he meant and that he would enable me to write them down utilising his writing experience.

So I wrote another short story, which Gordon liked, and then he suggested we write a book together. Meanwhile, however, he moved to Dartmoor with his wife – I think times were difficult for him and his family – right to the middle of nowhere. One day, while Gordon was away from home for a short time, a prisoner escaped from the nearby jail. Gordon was naturally concerned for the safety of his wife in the house on her own and he came up with an idea: to what lengths would a wife go to protect her home? The result was a novel called *The Siege of Trencher's Farm* (Gordon wrote it in ten days and had it published under a pseudonym) that was turned into the 1971 film *Straw Dogs*, starring Dustin Hoffman and Susan George and directed by Sam Peckinpah. Gordon earned a small fortune.

He came back to London and started watching me play again. During one match, I was about to take a throw-in when Gordon, who could virtually touch me from where he was standing, called out from the crowd, 'What do you think about doing that book now then?' We got thinking. We came up with *They Used to Play on Grass*.

Just after that incident my daughter Tracey was born. Worryingly, the hospital tag on her wrist fell off. After the event, I went home and over a glass of wine started thinking: what would you do if your baby was inadvertently swapped with someone else's or, just as tragically, they were swapped deliberately; if you discovered that your child was in fact in America or some other part of the world? You had stayed in East London but your child had gone to America with the wrong parents. Would you want the baby you had been left with or the child that was genetically yours? It's a difficult question because I reckon the truth is that you would want both. We had a real tear-jerking story on our hands. But written by cynical swines like Gordon and me, it just didn't work.

So we came up with *Hazell*. And it worked. It gave me a whole new perspective on life away from football. I was still in my early twenties and I had only lived for football. Suddenly there were doors opening to another way of life. Gordon taught me so much, about life aside from the game, about how to think more laterally. The experience also helped me think about football in a different way.

RIGHT: **With Gordon Williams in one of the goals at QPR's Loftus Road ground around 1971.**

Malcolm Allison has a great Gordon Williams story. Gordon would occasionally get seriously drunk and one night he and Malcolm were out for dinner together. Malcolm was quite sober when Gordon just fell head-first into his soup. He eventually got Gordon home. After dragging him across London and carrying him up to his front door, the two of them were greeted by a woman standing at the top of the stairs like Lady Macbeth. She screamed, 'Gordon, get that drunken man out of the house!' Some reception for Malcolm after he had sweated blood trying to carry his mate halfway across town!

I owe Gordon such a lot.

Bobby Keetch

Larger Than Life

T HE PHRASE 'LARGER THAN LIFE' WAS INVENTED WITH BOB IN MIND. HE WAS MY GREAT FRIEND, A FRIEND IN THE TRUE SENSE – BACKING YOU UP, ADVISING YOU, ALWAYS READY TO STAND AT YOUR SHOULDER WHEN YOU NEEDED SOMEONE YOU COULD TRUST.

He wasn't necessarily there to tell you what you wanted to hear, but he was always there. When I had my problems at Tottenham with Alan Sugar, and his pals were trying to make life hell for me, there wasn't a day when Bobby wasn't on the telephone. He'd suggest we meet up, have a drink and a meal. He'd drag me back to life.

Describing Bobby as an extraordinary person somehow does him scant justice. He was big and jovial and generous. He tried hard to be a success at everything he did. He was involved in deals everywhere and anywhere. He used to spend a lot of time in bed, making telephone calls, taking notes, etc., trying to set up deals before going out for lunch. A window cleaner was a

BELOW: **Wearing the blue and white hoops of QPR, February 1968.**

regular at the house and used to see him lying there. After a few months of this he said to Jan, Bob's wife, 'It must be very difficult for you with him being so crippled. How did it happen, an accident?'

Bobby wasn't exactly a failure in business, but if he wasn't as successful as he would have liked he never let it change his attitude to life, or let it get him down. He was at home with everybody: royalty and politicians, well-known celebrities and people who didn't have two pennies to rub together. He didn't care who they were or where they came from. When Bobby was around he made you feel good. He was the friend you were always glad to see.

I first met him when we were kids training at West Ham. Even then, all those years ago, he possessed a personality that charmed everyone who came into contact with him. It wasn't forced, it was

> When Bobby was around he made you feel good. He was the friend you were always glad to see.

just the way he was. He liked people and they, in turn, couldn't get enough of him. He was a decent player, no better than that, in a hard era and played for Fulham with Johnny Haynes, who adored him, and against the likes of Denis Law. I have to say Bob didn't take football too seriously. He would cause havoc at training with little scams the Fulham managers, Vic Buckingham and Bill Dodgin, never knew about – or maybe chose to ignore. For him, the game of football was a means to an end. In that sense he

ABOVE: **A firm challenge on no less than George Best, Fulham versus Manchester United, March 1964.**

was an anti-hero, someone who saw the game for what it was. He looked god-like, but he never wanted to be one.

I could tell a thousand stories about Bobby, and the thing is all of them would have a funny ending. He loved to laugh, even more so if it was at his own expense. Bobby had a lot of the playboy in him and he was a regular down the King's Road before the rest of us knew that was where it was all going to happen. He was a leader; he was our Sergeant Bilko. He and another mate, Ronnie Belton, used to stand outside Buckingham Palace when they were young taking photographs of American tourists. I don't know if there was actually film in the camera (I suspect not), but I can see them now, with a tousled old parrot showing no perceptible signs of life sitting on Ronnie's shoulder. Bobby told me that parrot moved only once in all the time they had it, and that was to pull a wart it thought was a peanut off the side of a tourist's face.

FACT FILE

FULL NAME: *Robert David Keetch*

BORN: *25 October 1941, Tottenham*

DIED: *29 June 1996 (aged 54)*

PLAYING CAREER

CLUBS: *West Ham United (as an amateur) 1957–59; Fulham 1959–66; Queens Park Rangers 1966–68*

APPEARANCES/GOALS: *West Ham United, no appearances; Fulham 106/2; QPR 49(3)/0*

CAREER TOTAL: *155(3) appearances/2 goals*

CLUB HONOURS: *Fulham, promotion from Second Division (as runners-up) 1958-59; QPR, Third Division Champions 1966–67; Promoted from Second Division 1967–68*

Bob and I had dinner together on the Friday after England were beaten by Germany in the Euro 96 semi-final. It was my last match in charge. Bob died the next day. He left us with lots of happy and wonderful memories.

Dave Coney

My First Idol

D
AVE CONEY LIVED IN THE SAME STREET THAT I WAS RAISED AND HE WAS PROBABLY THE FIRST PER-
SON TO MAKE A GREAT IMPRESSION ON ME. I WAS BROUGHT UP IN DAGENHAM IN EAST LONDON
AND WHEN I WAS YOUNG WE MOVED TO BONHAM ROAD.

This road ran parallel to a dual-carriageway called Valence Avenue where my nan and grandad lived.

I had a fantastic childhood, I must admit. I enjoyed pretty much everything about it, from my parents and grandparents to where we lived. I can remember that from an early age the only thing I wanted to be was a footballer. We were very lucky then in that there were very few cars around – in fact, in our particular road there weren't any cars – so we played football safely in the street. We also kicked a ball around in Valence Park which was in the next street up from ours. The park had acres of grass and ten tall trees. Between these trees and the bandstand was where the games always took place.

I think it's important to have that freedom. One great obstacle for kids today is that they have much less outdoor space to play in. They tend to spend much more time in their bedrooms watching television or playing computer games. I don't think that's healthy. To me, a vital element of growing up is play-ing with other kids, interacting with them, learning to give and take, to be part of a team. You learn valu-able lessons for later in life. It's so important to learn how to mix well with people and this can only be done through first-hand experience.

The people who played in the street were all from neighbouring houses and schools. Across the way from our house lived Dickie Walker who was captain of West Ham in the forties and fifties and then became a scout for Spurs. Dickie was an influential person in my life. Les Allen and his brothers lived in the house opposite – Les played for Chelsea,

Tottenham and QPR; his younger brother Dennis for Charlton, Reading and Bournemouth. Ken Brown, who played almost 400 games for West Ham from 1952 to 1966, lived in the area as well. Although not part of our street games, Jimmy Greaves, Bobby Moore and Martin Peters were also brought up local-ly. Then there were the Coney brothers – John, Eddie and Dave.

As I've said, Dave made a big impact on me. He had a great sense of humour and a terrifically posi-tive outlook on life. I was sure he would become a professional footballer. He captained the Spurs youth team and looked destined for great things, but he never signed for Spurs. I don't really know why, although I was told that his wish was to go into the family plastering business.

I used to play with Dave in all the games out on the streets. It was great practice for me because all the other boys were much older (they were about 14, I was only 11), but the experience helped me enormously and I found it much easier making the transition to playing in school matches, alongside my long-time pals Ron Hanley and Peter Auger.

A great many footballers came out of that one street in Dagenham. It was a strongly working class area and although we didn't have too much we did-n't lack for anything either. I was delighted Dave's son Dean went on to become a professional with Norwich and QPR. But Dave was my idol. He stood out from the crowd. At that time in my life, he was exactly who I wanted to be.

OPPOSITE: **Dave Coney leads out non-league Bedford Town in 1964.**

Ken Jones

The Doyen of Sports Writers

K EN JONES COMES FROM A LONG LINE OF FOOTBALLERS. I GUESS HIS FAMILY COULD BE CALLED A 'FOOTBALL ARISTOCRACY'. ON EITHER SIDE OF THE WAR – FROM 1919 TO 1970 – THE JONES FAMILY COULD CLAIM AN UNBROKEN 51 YEARS DURING WHICH AT LEAST ONE OF ITS MEMBERS WAS A LEAGUE FOOTBALLER.

Ken's father, Emlyn, was a league player with Merthyr Town, Southend United and Everton, and had four footballing brothers. One of them, Bryn, was an inside-forward who was transferred from Wolves to Arsenal in 1938 for a then record fee of £14,000, as a replacement for the legendary Alex James who had just retired. Unfortunately, the war interrupted his career and prevented Bryn from reaching his potential, although he won 17 Welsh caps.

Another of Ken's uncles, Ivor, played for Swansea and West Bromwich Albion. Ivor's son, Cliff Jones, was a vital part of Tottenham's Double side of 1961. Cliff Jones was one of Wales' finest players, winning 59 caps and scoring 16 goals. Cliff's grandson is presently on Tottenham's books.

Ken himself played as a professional until he was about 27, for Southend United, Gravesend and Northfleet, Swansea Town (now City) and Hereford United, without making any first class appearances. Ken did, though, obtain his coaching badge.

RIGHT: **Ken Jones (left) interviews the great Pele in Santos, Brazil, 1974.**

In September 1958 Ken joined the *Daily Mirror* as a football writer and became the paper's chief sports writer. When I was first in the Chelsea team I became good friends with George Graham, Ken Jones and Brian James of the *Daily Mail*. As far as journalists are concerned, Ken and Brian stood out because they were genuinely nice guys who never took any short cuts on the route to being good

writers – they simply relied on their genuinely outstanding writing ability. They didn't bad-mouth professional footballers and their articles were always even-handed. We got on very well.

The relationship with Ken in particular was helped by the fact that my mother was from Wales, so we had some common ground. In fact, I was evacuated to Wales during the war and the family always went back there for the school holidays.

Ken and I have been friends ever since. If I had a problem I would call on Ken for advice. If he needed

an opinion on something he would contact me. We've always been very close. I'm proud to say that I liked him and his family then and I like them now – Ken hasn't changed at all. He'll never let you down.

Unfortunately, a few years ago Ken had a terrible accident. He was going to a Christmas party where he expected to have a drink so he purposely didn't take his car. He had planned to go home on the train. As he arrived at the station, his train was pulling away and he fell between the carriages and on to the rails. His arm was severed.

Ken had always been something of a hypochondriac, a bit of a worrier. My instant reaction to the

I've got great admiration for Ken and his sports writing.

dreadful news was to wonder, how on earth is he going to react to this? I went to visit him in hospital the next day and was amazed to find him laughing and joking with some friends. I thought he must still be in shock. I asked him how he was and he said, 'Fine, absolutely fine.' Ken's never changed to this day. He enjoys life to the full (he now writes for the *Independent*) and plays a mean game of one-handed golf. In fact, he's just never come out of the shock, if that's what it was!

We meet up now for drinks and lunch and we're always on the phone to each other. I've got great admiration for Ken and his sports writing. He's invariably fair and he's never had to compromise his principles to get to the top. He's got there through sheer ability and a wonderful knowledge of the game.

FACT FILE

FULL NAME: *Kenneth Powell Jones*

BORN: *11 October 1931, Merthyr Tydfil*

PLAYING CAREER

CLUBS: *Southend United; Gravesend and Northfleet; Swansea Town (now City); Hereford United (pre-Football League)*

Dick Foss

Superb at Nurturing Talent

Dick Foss was a pre-war wing-half at Stamford Bridge and, like many others of his era, the war took away Dick's best playing years. During the hostilities he turned out frequently for Chelsea, making more than 200 appearances.

These included two Wembley finals in the South League Cup, which Chelsea won in 1944/45. But after the war Dick played only sporadically and retired in 1947 aged 35.

That same year Dick was taken on to Chelsea's coaching staff and five years later he was appointed the club's youth team manager. The appointment was made by Chelsea's new manager Ted Drake – the former Arsenal centre-forward could see the value of nurturing talent from within. By the time I got to work with Dick, the man was a legend. He had an unglamorous job but he was hugely valued as the coach primarily responsible for Chelsea's future success. We all thought the world of him, and of his knack of teaching young players the game's skills.

Chelsea won the FA Youth Cup two years in a row in 1960 and 1961, beating Preston North End and Everton in the respective finals. Shortly after this, the club were relegated from the First Division and several members of the youth team whom Dick Foss had nurtured found themselves straight into the first team. (It wasn't the first time that a crop of Dick's young charges had taken this upward step into the senior team.) At this time his youth side included Barry Bridges, Jimmy Greaves, Mel Scott, Ken Shellito, Bobby Tambling, Ron and Allan Harris, Micky Block, Mike Harrison, Peter Bonetti, John Hollins, Bert Murray, Peter Houseman, David Cliss, Peter Brabrook and many other well-known Chelsea starlets. They were all very promising players.

One of Dick's outstanding characteristics was his terrific 'manner' with his players. He knew how to

have fun – he always had a twinkle in his eye and a cheeky, saucy sense of humour – but he also had a great sense of discipline and a wonderful sense of elegance and style. If you wanted to be in his team you did not break his rules. He created an excellent working atmosphere and he was a great leader. The result was consistently good results with all his teams. I more than enjoyed working with him.

Dick was also very loyal. Just after I left to go to Spurs, he spoke very well about me at a function that was attended by Chelsea's manager Tommy Docherty. Dick was sacked shortly after this and I think it had something to do with Dick supporting me even though I had fallen out with Docherty. Tommy didn't feel that was right. It was a great pity because Dick was an absolutely crucial element of Chelsea's

success. As far as I'm concerned, the club was petty to get rid of a man who had spent so long at Chelsea, who had dedicated so much of his career to bringing through talented individuals (at a great success rate) who would go on to make a crucial contribution to the first team.

In fact, I don't know any player who was at Chelsea around this time who wasn't indebted to Dick. He was the master of all he surveyed and I believe he was also a key figure in the general development of the game after the war, helping to bring football into the modern era. In a way, the great work that Dick did at Chelsea in the fifties and sixties contributed to the strength of the national side and to the success that culminated in the 1966 World Cup.

The key ingredient in Dick's teaching methods was the ability to make football a joy to participate in. He created a fantastically fertile atmosphere in which boys wanted to play every day. Dick is one of the people who I have always greatly respected.

Jimmy Thompson

Crazy Dedication

THEY DON'T MAKE THEM LIKE JIMMY ANY MORE, AND WHILE THOSE WHO CAME UNDER HIS SPELL WILL PROBABLY SAY 'THANK HEAVENS!' THEY WILL ALSO BE THE FIRST TO SAY HOW MUCH THEY OWE HIM. JIMMY THOMPSON HAD A PROFOUND EFFECT ON A LOT OF YOUNGSTERS LIKE MYSELF WHO WANTED TO BE PROFESSIONAL FOOTBALLERS.

He was the Chelsea scout in my area of London, and it was Jimmy who convinced me to join the club.

He is best described as an English eccentric. He was certainly outrageous, and I don't think he would object, were he still around, if I said that when I first got to know him I thought he was as mad as a March hare. His behaviour and the way he dressed was certainly different to anything I'd experienced before. But he took a genuine interest in our futures and that's why lads like myself grew to like and trust him.

There were occasions when I could have done without his advice, however, like the time when I was laid up after I had damaged an ankle badly enough to keep me out of a London schoolboy trial. Jimmy would have none of it and turned up with a 'miracle balm' in a bottle. He explained in a whisper that it was so secret it was banned. 'Only top professionals can get hold of it,' he said, then added with a wink, 'After this you'll be back on your feet playing.' He took off his trilby – an event in itself – put his jacket behind a chair, rolled up his sleeves and massaged my bad foot and ankle for two solid hours, during which time it turned black. 'Get a ball,' he then said, 'take it into the back and try kicking it. I don't mean a pass – put everything into the shot.' 'But I can't stand,' I spluttered. 'Do it!' he ordered. I did as he said, and fainted with the pain. I was taken to hospital where the doctors diagnosed my injury as a broken bone in the foot that Jimmy had been massaging.

Jimmy surrounded you with a crazy warmth. He was kind, funny and mad, and I won't forget him.

Cliff Lloyd

Dedicated to Progress

AFTER A MODEST PLAYING CAREER SPANNING EITHER SIDE OF THE WAR, CLIFF LLOYD BECAME SEC-
RETARY OF THE PLAYER'S UNION – THE PROFESSIONAL FOOTBALLERS' ASSOCIATION – IN 1953. HE
DEDICATED HIS CAREER TO ACHIEVING PROGRESS FOR PROFESSIONAL FOOTBALLERS.

Cliff was a great character who was admired and loved throughout the country. He was a real fighter and won many battles with the football hierarchy on behalf of the players. Virtually all the benefits enjoyed by players today can be attributed to Cliff Lloyd. He achieved a huge amount as a football administrator and as the PFA's chief negotiator. Working closely with the PFA Chairman Jimmy Hill, Cliff was a key figure in forcing the removal of the unfair maximum wage, a challenge that was only upheld after very long and drawn-out negotiations with the Football League. Johnny Haynes went on to become the first £100-a-week player.

Cliff and Jimmy had further negotiations with the League and the Ministry of Labour to achieve players' freedom of contract and remove the ties that virtually bound a player to one club for life. This was a massive step forward because players were now free to negotiate a fairer deal. Previously, clubs had effectively held players to ransom and this simply wasn't fair. Cliff was very determined to change the clubs' standard contractual terms so that players were treated well and earned the right to play for whichever club they wanted, and at a decent wage.

I have worked on the PFA committee in my time, and I've also been the PFA's Vice-Chairman. Maurice Setters, Gordon Taylor and Derek Dougan were on the committee too and I remember vividly how Maurice and I always used to make Cliff Lloyd laugh. We could make him cry, his eyes would go red and he'd have to get out a handkerchief to stop crying. We enjoyed ourselves on the committee but we also got things done – to me, that's the ideal combination.

Cliff was enormously knowledgeable about all aspects of the sport, particularly about events off the pitch. He knew the ins-and-outs of the game, what you could and couldn't do as a manager or as a referee. He knew the intricacies of the 'business' of football. You always felt much more educated about a subject once you'd had a conversation with Cliff.

He was a very fair man and would support the players, but not for the sake of it. If he felt the players were in the wrong over a particular issue, he would tell them he couldn't support them on that point. Cliff had a very keen sense of what was right and what was wrong.

Cliff was a wonderful story teller and I recall one story in particular that illustrates the attitude of the era he played in. Because money was so tight in the game at this time, all the players' bootlaces would be collected up at the end of each match, washed and then given out again in time for the next game. Everything had to be used to its full value.

Cliff twisted his ankle badly just 15 minutes into a game one day, and so he was carried off the pitch and laid on a table in the dressing room. Just as he was being put down, the crowd roared outside so the two men who had brought him in ran out to see who had scored. They forgot about poor old Cliff and left him there on the table in the dressing room with his ankle swelling by the second. He was in agony.

The team came in at half-time 1-0 down and the manager paced around the table giving the players a stern talking-to. Nobody took any notice of Cliff,

whose ankle was so swollen by this time that it was about to burst. No-one offered to undo his laces or take his boot off. Then the players disappeared for the second half, leaving him still helpless on the table. On their return to the dressing room at the end of the game, Cliff's team-mates were all quiet because they'd lost. Finally Cliff said, 'Is there any chance of someone taking my boot off?' The team's physio looked at the boot and realised that it was not going to come off that easily anymore. The ankle has swollen so much that he couldn't get the knots in the laces undone. Cliff then said to the physio, 'Just cut the laces.' That was the cue for the physio to turn to the manager and say, 'How are we off for laces?' Obviously, the laces had the edge in importance over players in those days.

Gordon Taylor is now the Secretary of the PFA

and Cliff Lloyd taught him the ropes. Cliff must have done a good job because Gordon has excelled at the role too.

All modern-day players owe Cliff an enormous debt. As well as breaking the maximum wage and achieving freedom of contract for players, he set up education funding to enable youngsters to gain qualifications to secure their futures outside the game. Cliff also instigated accident funds for players who are forced to retire following injury, and he set up a benevolent fund so that players can be cared for in their old age. He ensured that players are able to receive medical treatment and financial aid after they finish playing.

Cliff sadly died in January 2000 but he handed down a fantastic legacy to modern players.

Cliff Lloyd was a quiet man. He was loved by all those who worked with him.

Danny Blanchflower

Self-belief in Abundance

DANNY BLANCHFLOWER NEVER LOOKED LIKE A FOOTBALLER. HE RESEMBLED A MEMBER OF THE ARISTOCRACY OR AN ACCOUNTANT. HE SEEMED DIFFERENT FROM THE OTHER PLAYERS. THEY ALL LOOKED AS IF THEY'D HAD A TOUGH LIFE AND A TOUGH TIME OF IT GETTING TO THE TOP, BUT DANNY GAVE THE IMPRESSION THAT HE HAD JUST STEPPED OUT OF UNIVERSITY. (IN FACT, DANNY WAS A GRADUATE OF ST ANDREW'S UNIVERSITY.)

Blanchflower was always my hero at Spurs, along with Johnny Brooks and Dave Mackay. Danny was an inspirational leader and also one of the finest footballers ever to wear the famous white shirt. He combined graceful movements with remarkable skill. His game was about subtlety and speed of thought, about awareness and perception that allowed interception before confrontation – although he defended

was as legendary as the grace of his play. There were many different facets to Danny Blanchflower. He was a realist but also a romantic, a winner but always a private man, he loved playing and talking about football, and football loved him.

He was, of course, one of the most famous players in Spurs' history and his influence

BELOW: **Danny in full flight for Tottenham Hotspur in March 1958.**

> ## If he was still around today, Danny would detest the media's obsession with the private lives of sports stars.

well when the occasion demanded. I think the perfection of Danny's passing will always remain as a vivid memory. His best pass was hit from the right side of midfield, lofted 35 yards into the inside-left position. It posed a constant threat to the opposition. Although he was never particularly fast, his intelligence was ample compensation.

Danny embodied the finest principles of sportsmanship within his own doctrine of how things should be done. He had a noble air. He was also a great thinker about the game, both on and off the field, and was a marvellous character whose humour

will live on forever at White Hart Lane. A great many fans still remember Danny's remarkable skills. In his case, it is impossible to exaggerate – he really was as good as all the legends would have us think.

With Blanchflower at the helm, in 1961 Spurs were the first team in the twentieth century to win the League and FA Cup Double, an achievement that was previously thought impossible. The following year Ipswich and Burnley edged them out of the title race in a season which, at one stage, looked like it might bring the Treble of League, FA Cup and European Cup. In the end, the club had to settle for 'just' the FA Cup and third place in the League.

Danny gave the impression that he had just stepped out of university.

The 1962/63 season brought second place in the League (behind Everton) and the European Cup-Winners' Cup. It was a golden era for Tottenham.

Danny was nominally the club's captain, but he enjoyed significantly more influence over the team than is normally the case. He was virtually the manager on the field. Spurs' actual manager, Bill Nicholson, allowed Danny his free run so that his undoubted leadership qualities could be exploited fully.

Such was Bill Nicholson's faith and, it has to be said, complete unselfishness, that he did precisely what was best for the team because he was not threatened at all by Danny. In fact, Nicholson and Blanchflower used to thrash out team tactics together at training sessions. On the pitch Danny was free to make changes as he saw fit, as the state of the game demanded. The players all recognised his leadership qualities and responded to his commands without any dissension.

But neither was the manager's authority ever called into question. It was a unique situation and one that I think would be difficult to repeat today. If a player got too dominant nowadays, the media would be running stories claiming the manager was about to be sacked. In reality, a close player/manager

relationship can be very useful. After all, it is the players who are on the pitch, not the manager. As much as he might like to interfere, the manager can only direct proceedings from the bench in a very limited capacity. It is a huge plus point for a boss to have a skipper out there on the pitch who has a voice and a brain that can take responsibility.

I have seen players take on this role – Michel Platini is an example – but it has to be a very special relationship

ABOVE: **Casting a critical eye over his footwear in the White Hart Lane boot room in September 1958.**

between player and manager for the former to understand how the latter is thinking. The player must be absolutely clear on when he has to defer to his manager in order to avoid conflicts either on or off the pitch.

It is funny, but Danny's early footballing days did nothing to suggest the greatness that was to come. After a couple of seasons with Barnsley he demanded a move, partly because he was unable to persuade manager Angus Seed that the players would benefit from practising with a ball during training. The same went for Chelsea when I first joined the club. I enjoyed more practice with a ball at school than I did at my first professional club! There was a school of thought at the time, not supported by anyone with any intelligence it has to be said, that if the players did not see a ball all week they would be hungry for it when Saturday came around.

Danny did not achieve major international honours (and neither did Angus Seed!), but he was very proud to be Northern Irish and led his team to the 1958 World Cup finals where they reached the quarter-final stage – an outstanding achievement which owed much to his leadership and inspirational qualities.

His original club, Glentoran, are immensely proud of their former player. On the occasion of the Football League's centenary season in 1998/99, a committee of football historians selected Danny as one of the hundred most influential players in English football. Two more former Glentoran players, Jimmy McIlroy (Burnley) and Peter Doherty (Manchester City, Derby County and Huddersfield Town), were also included. The club were delighted.

Danny's brother Jackie was in the Manchester United team that was unfortunately involved in the Munich air crash. Even though Jackie survived, his injuries were such that he never played again. However, he did go on to make a very good and funny after-dinner speaker.

By the time I started out in management Danny's playing career had come to an end, but he used to write a column in the *Sunday Express* which was

FACT FILE

FULL NAME: *Robert Dennis Blanchflower*

BORN: *10 February 1926, Belfast*

DIED: *9 December 1993*

PLAYING CAREER
CLUBS: *Glentoran 1946–49; Barnsley 1949–51; Aston Villa 1951–54; Tottenham Hotspur 1954–63*

APPEARANCES/GOALS:

	League	FA Cup	European
Glentoran	128/7		
Barnsley	68/2	2/0	
Aston Villa	148/10	7/0	
Tottenham Hotspur	337/15	33/4	12/2

CAREER TOTAL: *735 appearances/40 goals*

HONOURS: *(all with Tottenham) First Division Champions 1960–61; FA Cup Winners 1961, 1962; European Cup-Winners' Cup Winners 1962–63; Footballer of the Year 1958, 1961 (Tottenham were the first club in the twentieth century to win the League/Cup 'Double' in 1961, and the first British club to win a European trophy in 1962–63.)*

INTERNATIONAL: *Northern Ireland 56 appearances/2 goals, 1950–63*

MANAGEMENT CAREER
CLUBS: *Chelsea 1978–79*

INTERNATIONAL: *Northern Ireland 1976–78*

BELOW: **Danny (left) enjoys a joke with Johnny Haynes, another of my Heroes.**

refreshingly thoughtful. Often he would come to interview me and we would sit and chat. I always found him fascinating to listen to and great company. He was one of life's teachers. He had this great quality of natural leadership. He made me feel: Yes, I know what he means, we could do this or that, and that would change the way the game is played.

Over the years I have learned the skills of management from many people. Danny was definitely one of the individuals who greatly influenced me as I embarked on my managerial career.

He also knew how to inspire. I've said many times that self-belief is worth a fair amount of talent. With self-belief, players can go that bit further, even further than their talents would normally allow, and Danny could make you think you could do anything you wanted. He also got the team working for each other, and would hold it together if things looked like they were going downhill. In fact, with Danny it was much more likely that the opposition would fall apart and not his team. If you knew that you were faced with Danny Blanchflower on the opposing team, you really had something to worry about. You knew that you were up against eleven men who were totally convinced they could beat you, and who had within their ranks a man who could organise them to achieve their goals. The passing and movement of that Spurs team was the best I've ever played against.

ABOVE: **Triumphantly lifting the FA Cup trophy in May 1961.**

But Danny was also a very private man and hated any intrusion into his privacy. (You couldn't possibly imagine him having a night out with Dave Mackay!) For example, take the filming of Danny's episode of *This is Your Life*. In those days it was filmed live. Bill Nicholson hated being away from the ground, but after much persuasion he had put work aside for a while and gone along to the studios. Nicholson, along with all the players, were gathered in a television studio, watching Eamonn Andrews approach Danny. Eamonn Andrews just got round to saying, 'Danny Blanchflower, this is your life', when Danny spun round and said 'No, it's not', and stalked off.

Nicholson was furious at what he considered to be a waste of his precious work time. The *This is Your Life* team were mortified. Apparently, shortly after this they started pre-recording the programme. Danny was the first person to refuse to go on the show. Really, whichever member of his family had been co-ordinating it should have known better – Danny was very private and he wasn't about to have his life displayed to the public. Whatever he had to hide, if anything, remained hidden. If he was still around today, he would detest the media's obsession into the private lives of sports stars. He was simply brought up in a very different era.

Danny was a realist and he knew the time had come to retire when, in the 1963/64 season, he was upstaged at Old Trafford by a young upstart by the name of Denis Law. Denis gave Danny the run-around, the Scotsman scoring a hat-trick in a 4-1 hammering for Spurs. That was that, and at the end of the season Danny called it a day. He had the sense to retire when he was still regarded as a great footballer. Judging when to hang up the boots is always difficult – there is always the temptation to keep going for just one more season, but fans often forget the great moments when they see a player struggling. Danny Blanchflower knew exactly when to go. He remains a true great in the hearts and minds of all Spurs fans.

I remember reading John Fennelly's obituary of Danny that was published in the Tottenham match-day programme. It was perfect. 'Those too young [to remember Danny] should listen to and believe the tales about the great man – because exaggeration is impossible when the subject is the genius of the great Danny Blanchflower.'

BELOW: **Danny watches Burnley's Jimmy Adamson toss a coin before the start of the 1962 FA Cup final.**

THE VENABLES VERDICT

- *Blanchflower didn't look like a footballer. More like a university graduate.*
- *His game was characterised by grace, skill, subtlety, awareness and a keen sense of sportsmanship.*
- *An inspirational leader with huge reserves of self-belief.*
- *Enjoyed a unique working relationship with manager Bill Nicholson.*
- *Led Spurs to the League and FA Cup Double in 1961.*

Cliff Jones

Underrated Speedster

A S A PLAYER, CLIFF JONES WAS EVERYTHING YOU WOULDN'T EXPECT FROM JUST LOOKING AT HIM – BEWILDERINGLY FAST AND, FOR A PLAYER BELOW AVERAGE HEIGHT (HE WAS 5 FEET 6 INCHES), OFTEN DEVASTATING IN THE AIR.

He was a key member of the great Tottenham Double side of the sixties, right up there with the likes of Dave Mackay and Danny Blanchflower, yet for a man who achieved so much I think it is fair to say he was underrated – though not by Spurs fans, in his native country or by those of us who had seen him destroy defenders with consummate ease.

> ### When I say he was quick, I mean *quick*. Either side he would be past you in a blur.

Cliff in full flight was quite an experience, for player and spectator alike. When I say he was quick, I mean *quick*. Either side he would be past you in a blur. When he was in his stride you couldn't stop him. If you were lucky you managed a touch of the ball. He had the same sort of pace as Real Madrid's little flyer Gento, either of whom you'd have put a bet on to beat an Olympic sprinter of the time. And as I have said, for a smallish man he could outjump the tallest, rangiest defender. In the air, Cliff was simply fantastic. Bobby Moore always regarded him as the most difficult of players to play against when crosses came in. As a defender Bobby, like all defenders, had to wait until the ball was at a height that made it acceptable to attack. If it was too high, forget it. It was when the ball was almost on Bobby's forehead that Cliff Jones would leap in, come across the front and take the ball.

Cliff comes not so much from a family as a footballing dynasty. His father was one of five brothers, all of whom played League football; indeed, they can claim to have had at least one of their number registered with the League for over 50 years. Cliff had all the talent necessary to make it to the very top with club and country, and he didn't disappoint, adding championships to a CV which includes domestic cup success and Tottenham's historic victory in the European Cup-Winners' Cup in 1963 – the first time an English club side had won a European trophy.

Jones cost Tottenham a record £35,000 from Swansea Town, as they were then called (the City came later) – a huge amount of money 42 years ago. Arsenal were the rivals for Cliff's services, but they thought the asking price too high and pulled out, leaving the door wide open for Spurs. It was a considerable error of judgement by the Gunners and a superb coup signing for their North London rivals.

THE VENABLES VERDICT

- *His game was characterised by bewildering pace. In full flight, he terrorised defences.*

- *Though below average height, he was often devastatingly effective in the air and outjumped even the tallest of opponents.*

- *A key member of Tottenham's 1960/61 Double side.*

- *In a ten-year career at White Hart Lane, won the League title, the FA Cup three times and the European Cup-Winners' Cup.*

- *Capped 59 times for Wales, scoring 16 times. Played in 1958 World Cup quarter-finals.*

ABOVE: **Cliff (left) celebrates after team-mate Alan Gilzean (hidden) scores past Sheffield Wednesday goalkeeper Ron Springett, September 1967.**

FACT FILE

FULL NAME: *Clifford William Jones*

BORN: *7 February 1935, Swansea*

PLAYING CAREER

CLUBS: *Swansea Town (now City) 1952-58; Tottenham Hotspur 1958-68; Fulham 1968-69; non-league football with King's Lynn, Wealdstone, Bedford Town, Cambridge City and Wingate FC.*

APPEARANCES/GOALS:

	League	FA Cup	FL Cup	European
Swansea Tn.	168/47	9/1		
Tottenham	314(4)/135	35(4)/16	2/1	19/7
Fulham	23(2)/2		1/0	

CAREER TOTAL: *571(10) appearances/209 goals*

HONOURS: *First Division Champions 1960-61; First Division runners-up 1962-63; FA Cup Winners 1961, 1962, 1967; European Cup-Winners' Cup Winners 1963*

INTERNATIONAL: *Wales 59 appearances/16 goals, 1954-70; played in quarter-finals of 1958 World Cup*

Cliff will agree that his greatest moment was scoring a hat-trick for Spurs when they overwhelmed Polish champions Gornik Zabrze at White Hart Lane. It was one of those stunning European nights when everything is just perfect: the crowd, the atmosphere and the result. Furthermore, for Cliff and Spurs it was the opportunity to avenge what had been a dreadful first-leg match in Poland. They'd had a nightmare journey to Poland and been forced to stay in a flea-ridden hotel. It all ended up with Cliff and *The Times'* football correspondent Geoffrey Green having a difference of opinion with the over-zealous local police. Both Cliff and Geoffrey were jailed, but very briefly. The result, a 4-2 defeat, was bad enough to suggest that Tottenham's chances of survival were worse than grim, but they went on to that stunning victory, Cliff bagging three in an 8-1 thrashing (aggregate 10-5). The crowd was in intimidating form that night, letting the Poles know exactly what they thought of them for the way in which Tottenham had been treated two weeks earlier.

Cliff retired in December 2000 after over twenty years as a PE teacher at Highbury Grove School, but the Jones name in football may live on as his grandson is now playing for one of Spurs' junior sides.

Jimmy Hill

A Man For All Seasons

JIMMY IS INCLUDED IN MY BOOK OF HEROES NOT AS A FOOTBALLER BUT AS A MAN FOR ALL SEASONS. HE IS ONE OF THOSE PEOPLE WHO JUST EXUDES CONFIDENCE AND NON-STOP ENTHUSIASM. HE WAS A GOOD – THOUGH NOT OUTSTANDING – PLAYER AS AN INSIDE-FORWARD, BUT SELF-ASSURANCE TOOK HIM TO THE TOP.

I recall one incident that summed it all up. Jimmy was playing with Fulham at the time. The team were not playing very well so the crowd started booing a particular player. Jimmy went up to Johnny Haynes and said that the crowd's reaction wasn't right and it wouldn't be good for this player's morale. He never dreamed for one moment that the supporters were booing him. Typical Jimmy. His level of confidence

> **Self-belief gets you everywhere and it certainly did in Jimmy's case.**

made him a better player. Self-belief gets you everywhere and it certainly did in Jimmy's case.

He is best known as a television personality but his areas of interest are far wider than that. He originally planned to be a stockbroker, but national service in 1946 forced a change of career. He had hoped that his talent as a Boy's Brigade cornet player would get him into the regimental band. The band leader was not impressed with him – but then it was the great Johnny Dankworth.

In the army he found himself playing in a side with nine professionals, and that awakened in him the belief that he could earn his living playing football. After playing with Folkestone Town in the Kent League, he approached Ted Drake, then manager at Reading, but Drake was not prepared to offer him professional terms. However, Brentford took him on in 1949, and Jimmy played three seasons there alongside Ron Greenwood, from whom he learned a great deal about the game.

In 1951 Fulham indicated that they were interested in his services, just as they were

LEFT: Jimmy bravely beats the Doncaster Rovers goalkeeper to the ball at Craven Cottage in April 1957.

about to be relegated from the First Division. Jimmy remained with Fulham for the remainder of his playing career, teaming up with the legendary Johnny Haynes.

Jimmy has never been afraid to express his views, and during a match one Saturday afternoon a heavily-bearded Hill was constantly giving vocal advice to

FACT FILE

FULL NAME: *James William Thomas Hill, OBE*

BORN: *22 July 1928, Balham*

PLAYING CAREER

CLUBS: *Folkestone Town (as an amateur); Reading (as an amateur); Brentford 1949–52; Fulham 1952–61*

APPEARANCES/GOALS: *Brentford 83/10; Fulham 276/41*

CAREER TOTAL: *359 appearances/51 goals*

HONOURS: *Second Division runners-up 1958–59*

PFA CAREER: *Chairman of the PFA 1957–1961*

MANAGEMENT CAREER

CLUBS: *Coventry City 1961–67*

HONOURS: *Third Division Champions 1963–64; Second Division Champions 1966–67*

MEDIA CAREER: *Head of Sport, LWT, 1967–73; BBC Match of the Day, 1973 onwards; Sky Sports interviewer*

George Cohen, later to become a World Cup winner in 1966. George was ignoring the bulk of this advice, much to Jimmy's annoyance, when from the stands came a voice using a mock Jewish accent: 'Cohen, Cohen, give the ball to the bloody rabbi when he tells you!' Needless to say, this caused much amusement, not least to Jimmy's mum and dad who were sitting in the stands.

I have a nice story about Jimmy from when we played a charity match in Ireland. It was English veterans against an Irish team. After the match we went to a function and found ourselves in this rather grand room with an Irish female entertainer. She asked for three assistants for her next act and she chose Jimmy Hill, Jimmy Greaves and myself. She wanted us to help her sing *Old Macdonald*. She told us that I was to be the dog, Greaves the cow and Jimmy Hill the duck. Jimmy looked a bit upset and I sidled over and asked him what was wrong. He said, 'Do me a favour and let me be the dog. I do a great dog!' Whatever he did, he wanted to be the best at it.

But Jimmy used his powers of persuasion to great effect when he improved his fellow players' circumstances. He became a committee member of the Professional Footballers' Association in 1955, and the PFA Chairman by 1957. His finest hour came in 1961 when – with Cliff Lloyd, the secretary of the PFA – he was instrumental in the removal of the maximum wage, which at that time was £20 a week during the season and £17 during the summer off-season. This was achieved only after protracted negotiations with the Football League. Later, the same Hill/Lloyd team would negotiate with the Ministry of Labour for the right of freedom of contract for the players.

Jimmy brilliantly represented George Eastham in a famous test case at the High Court after Newcastle

TOP LEFT: **That unmistakable face! Jimmy wearing the Fulham shirt with pride, March 1958.**

United had refused to allow the player to join Arsenal at the end of the contract, even though they also refused to allow Eastham to play for them. (Ernie Clay financed Eastham while he was not getting his wages.) The so-called 'slave contract' was abolished. Modern-day players, who are earning a fortune and have the right of freedom of movement between clubs, have much to thank Jimmy Hill and Cliff Lloyd for. Back then a player signed for a club and stayed for life – the club could pretty well treat him as they wished.

After becoming manager of Coventry when he retired from playing, Jimmy then became Chairman of the club in 1975, but not before he had stunned them by resigning as manager to become Head of Sport at London Weekend Television. With his usual indefatigable energy, he set about revolutionising televised football with his Sunday afternoon programme *The Big Match*.

He returned to his first love, Fulham, as Chairman for ten years from 1987. He survived the club's turmoil, steering it through choppy waters before Mohammed Al Fayed took over the reins.

There is one last anecdote about Jimmy that tells its own story. Arsenal were playing Liverpool at Highbury in September 1972 and Jimmy was commentating. A linesman tore a leg muscle so the call went out for a replacement. (No fourth official in those days!) Jimmy had got the necessary refereeing qualifications and he passed the microphone to a colleague before emerging on to the pitch. He handled the job like everything in his life – with consummate efficiency.

ABOVE: **That famous cameo role as a stand-in linesman at Highbury in September 1972.**

THE VENABLES VERDICT

- *Whatever Jimmy did, he wanted to be the best at it.*
- *Instrumental in the removal of the players' maximum wage in 1961.*
- *Today's players have much to thank him for.*
- *Played with Brentford and Fulham as an inside-forward.*
- *Managed Coventry and has been chairman of Coventry, Fulham and the PFA.*

Dave Sexton

A Great Teacher

DAVE SEXTON HAS RIGHTLY EARNED A REPUTATION AS ONE OF ENGLAND'S FINEST COACHES. HE IS ANOTHER PRODUCT OF THE 'ACADEMY OF FOOTBALL' FROM WHICH HAVE GRADUATED SUCH FREE THINKERS AS MALCOLM ALLISON, FRANK O'FARRELL, NOEL CANTWELL, TOMMY DOCHERTY AND JOHNNY BOND. THEY WERE ALL DESTINED TO BECOME LEAGUE MANAGERS AND INFLUENCE THE ENGLISH GAME.

The first time I met Dave Sexton was when I was playing for Chelsea and he came to the club as the reserve team coach. He was offered the job by Tommy Docherty. I got talking to Dave on the train one day and was really fascinated by what he had to say, his creative thinking on how you could approach the game and what you could do in certain situations. I was so fortunate to meet someone as professional and inspirational as Dave so early in my career as a pro. He provided the missing piece of the jigsaw. He started to bring the best out of me. I was then able to talk to other youth players and we became increasingly enthusiastic about learning new tactics and strategies as opposed to just going out there and playing football. Without doubt, it was Dave Sexton who got us interested in the game. He was responsible for a great many players moving into management later in their careers. I didn't agree with

> ## Dave was responsible for a great many players moving into management later in their careers.

what Dave did all the time, but he made me think differently and stimulated me into wanting to adapt and improve my ideas.

Dave liked a joke and was very easy going … until you upset him, then he had a real temper. I remember Peter Osgood upset him once and Dave offered him the chance to go outside and sort it out with a fight. Peter Osgood just said, 'I'm not that

stupid!' – Dave's father Archie was a champion heavyweight boxer.

Dave and I renewed our relationship later when we worked with England. He was the manager of the Under-21 side between 1981 and 1984 and I was the coach. (Dave's four-year reign at Manchester United was drawing to a close just as I was getting my teeth into the QPR job.) With the Under-21 team we won the European Championship in 1982, beating a very strong West Germany side in the final. That was certainly one of the highlights of our partnership.

BELOW: **Dave signs autographs outside Stamford Bridge in October 1967, early in his Chelsea management career.**

THE VENABLES VERDICT

• *A great teacher with the gift of being able to effectively communicate his message to the whole squad.*

• *Not totally comfortable with the wider role of manager. Would have preferred to be purely a coach.*

• *As manger of the England Under-21 side for many years, was responsible for bringing many household names through to the senior national team.*

• *Still involved in the England set-up, working alongside Sven-Goran Eriksson.*

ABOVE: **In the claret and blue of West Ham United during Dave's playing career, 1953.**

A lot of future England players came through our hands during this time – Bryan Robson, Peter Barnes, Kenny Sansom, Viv Anderson, Peter Reid, Glenn Hoddle. Under-21 level became the nursery for the development of future talent.

Dave was a very forward thinking person. I remember that in the fifties he and his little group used to meet in a local café. They used salt and pepper pots to represent players and would run through their theories on the game, particularly after Hungary had famously exposed our game in 1953.

He was a natural teacher and, like all good teach-

ers, he didn't really get the credit he deserved. Dave taught me how to teach players and how to improve them and I always thought that was the yardstick of a coach's success. You can be the best player in the world, just by using your natural talent and applying determination and focus, but to be a good coach you have to be able to successfully transmit your thoughts to the players and get them to do exactly what you want. That is far from easy. I have seen coaches confuse players with too many theories and that shows on the pitch. I have also met many coaches who have struck me as very clever and I have thought, 'Yeah they know a lot'. Then I have walked away without learning anything from the session. Keeping it simple, that's the key. I always like to simplify things.

What is important is that everyone understands the message. It's pointless having the top three brains out of a squad of 20 players understanding what you have just said when the rest haven't taken it on board. A good teacher makes sure that the whole class understands. That is a real skill because the teacher has got to keep the interest of the top three who have understood immediately while also going through the information thoroughly enough for the others. It's no good taking an hour to bang the theory into the bottom end of the class to find the top end have got bored and let their brains wander off somewhere else.

One thing was sure about Dave, he had no

patience with journalists, apart from men like Ken Jones who were very professional and kept their comments to the game. In the main Dave felt that journalists did not really have the interests of the game at heart. Dave was a pure football man, through and through.

My impression is that Dave would have preferred to have stayed as a coach and not been a manager, having to deal with the media and other peripheral

> **I have seen coaches confuse players with too many theories and that shows on the pitch. Keeping it simple, that's the key. I always like to simplify things.**

business matters. But there was little money in coaching, so he had to move upwards to achieve a half-decent salary. But as time has moved on, Dave has ended up in the field he always wanted to stay in. He is now back to pure coaching and works alongside current England manager Sven-Goran Eriksson.

Dave is much better known than most managers because he has such a wide following, nationally and internationally. Coaches have such a lot of respect for him. He has been part of the England set-up for 20 years and I think his presence is vital to the progress of the national side. If England are to return to being a strong force in international football then they need Dave to provide the stability and consistency in the coaching process. Managers may come and go, but Dave remains. I think that is one reason why England still do well.

RIGHT: **Working with the England U-21 side alongside Howard Wilkinson, May 2000.**

Dave Sexton continues to make a remarkable contribution to the English game. That is a measure of the man – he never tires of new ideas and new ways of doing things. At the age of 70, he is as fresh as when I met him 40 years ago. There are very few men about whom you can say that. I have great admiration for Dave and all he has achieved.

FACT FILE

FULL NAME: *David James Sexton*

BORN: *6 April 1930, Islington*

PLAYING CAREER
CLUBS: *Chelmsford City, up to 1951; Luton Town 1951–52; West Ham Utd 1952–56; Leyton Orient 1956–57; Brighton & HA 1957–59; Crystal Palace 1959–60*

APPEARANCES/GOALS: *Luton Town 9/1; West Ham Utd 74/27; Leyton Orient 24/4; Brighton & HA 49/26; Crystal Palace 27/11*

CAREER TOTAL: *183 appearances/69 goals*

CLUB HONOURS: *Third Division (South) Champions 1957–58 (with Brighton & HA)*

MANAGEMENT/COACHING CAREER
CLUBS: *Chelsea (coach) 1961–65; Fulham (coach) 1965–66; Arsenal (coach) 1966–67; Chelsea (manager) 1967–74; QPR (manager) 1974–77; Man Utd (manager) 1977–81; Coventry City (manager) 1981–83; England (coach) 1981 to date (U-21 team manager 1981–84; Technical Director of the FA's National School 1984–89; England manager's coach 1994–98; youth coaching 1998 to date)*

HONOURS: *FA Cup Winners 1970 (Chelsea); European Cup-Winners' Cup Winners 1971 (Chelsea); First Division runners-up 1975–76 (QPR); First Division runners-up 1979–80 (Man Utd); FA Cup Finalists 1978–79 (Man Utd); UEFA Champions 1982 (England U-21); UEFA Champions 1984 (England U-21)*

Dave Mackay

The Tough-tackling Buccaneer

DAVE MACKAY WAS THE ARCHETYPAL HARD MAN. HE WAS IMMENSELY STRONG AND POSSESSED AN IN-BUILT WILL TO WIN. BOTH DAVE AND DANNY BLANCHFLOWER WERE IN THE TOTTENHAM TEAM THAT SECURED THE DOUBLE IN 1960/61.

But whereas Blanchflower always looked so graceful and in control, Mackay was a buccaneer, always crashing into tackles. It should never be forgotten, though, that Dave was also a very skilful player.

I remember Dave well from my Spurs days. When I went to White Hart Lane I guess I was the 'governor' of the team in the sense that I often

> ## In terms of spirit and talent, he will always remain one of the best footballers the game has seen.

dictated play. Dave was not getting any younger. On my first day we had a six-a-side game in the ball court. It was a right old rough-house. If you got caught in a corner of the hall, Dave would just fly at you and crush you against the wall. It was his way of testing you out.

One of his tricks was to dive on the floor with both feet apart so he could get the ball whichever way you went; and if you tried to nutmeg him he would land on the floor so you weren't able to stick the ball through his legs. I worked this out early on so I knew you had to pass him earlier than usual. This is exactly what I did the first time, and as I went past him Dave punched me right in the Niagara Falls! Ouch! I crumpled to a heap on the floor.

I thought that maybe this was just accidental on Dave's part but the second time I tried going past him he did exactly the same again. I turned round and punched him back. A fight ensued and the other players had to separate us. What a first day! After

training most of the squad went to the small pub across the road for a drink. Dave came over to me and we started talking. We've got on really well ever since.

Though explosive and dynamic in the first half of his career, Dave became a defensive half-back, the kind of player who made sure that the opposing team's danger-man was 'looked after'. But his fiercely competitive spirit often saw him surge forward out of defence and into the opposing penalty area. His bravery couldn't be questioned there either. He might have been a defender at heart, but his ferocious shot – particularly on his sweet left foot – brought him more than his fair share of

BELOW: **A typically committed challenge in April 1960.**

If you got caught in a corner of the hall, Dave would just fly at you and crush you against the wall. It was his way of testing you out.

goals during his career. He usually scored precisely when his team really needed it.

It remains a great mystery to me, and to many others, that Dave won only 22 Scottish caps. It seemed as if the national team's selectors deliberately went for home-based players, probably as a deterrent to prevent their star players earning their living in England. Of course, what the selectors ended up doing was shooting themselves in the foot because

they desperately needed their high-calibre players, and they certainly needed a Dave Mackay in the team.

Dave had the most amazing skills at his disposal. At Spurs, Eddie Baily – the first team coach under Bill Nicholson and a Tottenham legend in his own right – used to give us various exercises to perform during training, one of which was to chip the ball against a coloured line on the wall, trap it on the knee and then strike it against a different-coloured line, then control it with the chest and finally trap it with the opposite foot. Dave would calmly say, 'Do you mean like this, Eddie?', then proceed to go through the whole routine effortlessly

ABOVE: **Dave leaps over Spurs team-mates (from left to right) Cliff Jones, Ron Henry and Jimmy Greaves.**

before looking at the coach as if to say, 'That's easy.' Eddie Baily would just sneer at him while the rest of us were in awe as he performed to perfection every ball skill that was called out. Dave was just naturally gifted; everything came so easily.

Mackay was a star even before he came to Spurs. It is rare for any Scottish team to eclipse the 'Old Firm' of Celtic and Rangers, but Dave was instrumental in helping his home-town club, Edinburgh's Heart of Midlothian, to do just that. Within the space of just five seasons, Hearts won the Scottish League (1957/58), the Scottish Cup (1956) and the

BOTTOM RIGHT: **I can't keep the grin off my face as Alan Mullery celebrates with Dave after our 1967 FA Cup final win. Goalkeeper Pat Jennings is behind the three of us.**

> I think Dave Mackay's contribution to the famous 1960/61 Double at Spurs was gigantic.

Scottish League Cup twice (1954/55 and 1958/59). Dave was also Scottish Footballer of the Year in 1958. Quite an achievement.

I think Dave Mackay's contribution to the famous 1960/61 Double at Spurs was gigantic. His absolute control over the crucial midfield area gave Danny Blanchflower a free rein to release Tottenham's superb forwards. The team scored 115 League goals that season, the highest total since the Second World War, winning 31 of their 42 matches. Dave played 37

FACT FILE

FULL NAME: *David Craig Mackay*

BORN: *14 November 1934, Edinburgh*

PLAYING CAREER
CLUBS: *Heart of Midlothian 1952–59; Tottenham Hotspur 1959–68; Derby County 1968–71; Swindon Town 1971–72*

APPEARANCES/GOALS:

	League	FA Cup	FL Cup	European
Hearts	135/27	16/0	26/2	2/0
Tottenham Hotspur	268/42	33/4		17/5
Derby County	122/5	7/0	16/2	
Swindon Town	25(1)/1	1/0		

CAREER TOTAL: *668(1) appearances/88 goals*

CLUB HONOURS: *First Division Champions 1960–61; First Division runners-up 1961–62; FA Cup Winners 1961, 1962, 1967 (all with Tottenham); Second Division Champions 1968–69 (with Derby Co); Scottish League Champions 1957–58; Scottish Cup Winners 1956; Scottish League Cup Winners 1954–55, 1958-59 (all with Hearts); Scottish Footballer of the Year 1958; Footballer of the Year 1969*

INTERNATIONAL: *Scotland 22 appearances/4 goals, 1957–66*

MANAGEMENT CAREER
CLUBS: *Swindon Town 1971–72 (player-manager); Nottingham Forest 1972–73; Derby County 1973–76; Walsall 1977–78; Birmingham City 1989–91*

HONOURS: *First Division Championship 1974–75 (at Derby County)*

Dave Mackay shouted to me, 'Venables, have a kick of this ball. It's the only kick you're going to get once the game starts.'

times and scored four goals. Without question, he was a key factor in Tottenham's success.

Dave's 1961 FA Cup winner's medal made him a rarity in that he was a League and cup winner both north and south of the border. He also played in the triumphant FA Cup sides of 1962 and 1967. However, he missed Spurs' historic 1963 European Cup-Winners' Cup triumph in Rotterdam through

injury. Tottenham beat Atletico Madrid 5-1 to claim English football's first ever European trophy.

The night before the 1967 Cup final Bill Nicholson took us into the West End to see a film. It must've been a suitable choice because I remember it put everyone in the right mood for the combat ahead. The next morning Dave and I took a stroll down Piccadilly in the sunshine. We talked about the big game ahead and I will never forget just how super-confident Dave sounded. There were absolutely no doubts in his mind that he was going to lift the trophy.

That night the club threw

BELOW: **Brian Clough congratulates Dave after Derby County have been confirmed as Second Division champions, April 1969.**

- *An archetypal hard man, a tough-tackling buccaneer. Possessed of a fiercely competitive spirit.*
- *Naturally gifted and highly skilful. His left-foot shooting was ferocious.*
- *A great joker. Full of fun, both on and off the pitch.*
- *A key figure in the Tottenham Double-winning side of 1960/61.*
- *Won League titles and cups on both sides of the border.*
- *Joined a very select band of men who have won the League title as both a player and a manager.*

a celebration party at the Savoy. Dave had knocked back a fair few glasses of his favourite brew and I remember him shouting at the manager, 'Sit down, Bill. You're getting boring.' He also mischievously knocked our commemorative medals into the air at one point. Everyone had to scrabble around on the floor to retrieve them, with Dave laughing like a drain before being carried off to bed.

The Scotsman enjoyed some remarkable success in England but it was also in England that he experienced his worst defeat. In April 1961 the 'Auld Enemy' thumped Scotland 9-3 at Wembley. Dave's Spurs team-mate Bobby Smith scored twice and Jimmy Greaves (soon to be a team-mate) helped himself to a hat-trick.

In 1968 Dave's career was rejuvenated. Believing that at 34 Dave was past his best, Tottenham allowed Derby County's manager Brian Clough to take him to the East Midlands. Clough was in the process of bringing together a good young team at the Baseball Ground and he thought Mackay's qualities in defence would be just what his youngsters needed. Clough's judgement was right. Dave led Derby out of the Second Division in the 1968/69 season, as champions. As captain, Mackay had made all the difference.

Unfortunately, Dave just missed out on the big party at Derby when Clough's side won the First Division championship for the first time in their his-

tory in 1971/72. By this time he had moved to Swindon Town as player/manager, aware that his playing days were now almost over. He returned to the Baseball Ground when Derby were in disarray after Brian Clough and Peter Taylor had resigned as a result of Clough being taken to task by the Derby Chairman over outspoken comments on television. Mackay was managing arch-rivals Nottingham Forest, but surprisingly Forest agreed to let him go – I guess they realised his heart was still at Derby.

The decision was a good one for both Derby and Mackay. In the 1974/75 season the club clinched their second League title, finishing two points clear of Bob Paisley's Liverpool and Bobby Robson's Ipswich Town. At a stroke Dave became one of the very few men to who have won the League title as both a player and a manager. The list also includes Ted Drake, Bill Nicholson, Sir Alf Ramsey, Joe Mercer, Bob Paisley, Howard Kendall, Kenny Dalglish and George Graham.

By 1976 the wheels were beginning to come off at Derby County and Dave – fairly or not – got the blame and the sack. I know exactly how that feels; I've been in the managerial hot seat. Often it isn't fair on the manager: he has done an honest job yet still someone has to carry the can – and it's always the manager. Dave had short spells at both Walsall (1977-78) and Birmingham City (1989-91) but, to all intents and purposes, his managerial career was over. In terms of spirit and talent, he will always remain one of the best footballers the game has seen.

When I was a young captain of Chelsea and Tottenham's Double team were on the wane, I remember running on to the pitch to warm up before playing Spurs. Dave Mackay shouted to me, 'Venables, have a kick of this ball. It's the only kick you're going to get once the game starts.' That summed Dave up, and he could obviously see into the future too because his prediction was spot on. He was a talented, aggressive guy who was also a lot of fun and a great joker. I love a laugh and Dave was always full of fun, on and off the pitch. We had a great time at Spurs.

Bill Shankly

A Matter of Life and Death?

BILL SHANKLY WILL REMAIN ONE OF THE BIGGEST LEGENDS IN THE GAME, A MAN OF EXTREME PASSION TO WHOM FOOTBALL MEANT EVERYTHING. THERE HAS NEVER BEEN A GREATER CHARACTER; YOU JUST COULDN'T DELIGHT IN LIFE AS MUCH AS HE CLEARLY DID.

I never saw him play, but I know from those who did see him perform at Carlisle and Preston North End that he was a fine, fiercely competitive wing-half. He was also the man who recognised the talent of Tom Finney, which to be fair can't have been his most difficult task.

When he went to America he refused to change his watch to American time, saying that British time was the real time.

Bill came up the hard way. He was born in a tiny miner's cottage in the Ayrshire/Lanarkshire village of Glenbuck. He was one of five sons, all of whom became professional footballers (Bill's brother Bob coached Dundee to a championship in 1961/62), and five daughters, so life was tough. Football was the only alternative to a life down the pit. It is difficult today to understand just how important football was to those tiny communities where money was scarce and life was difficult. It was like a religion. Men and boys would play until ten every night. The village of Glenbuck was tiny with a population of about 500, but it spawned 50 professional footballers, eleven of whom played for Scotland.

LEFT: **During his playing days, in a Preston North End shirt, December 1946.**

After learning his football with Glenbuck Cherrypickers, Bill moved on to Cranberry before joining Carlisle United as a professional in July 1932. A year later he was signed by Preston North End, with whom he would see out his career, winning an FA Cup winner's medal in 1938 when Huddersfield Town were beaten 1-0 by a penalty scored in the last minute of extra time. Like many players of his era he lost seven years of his playing career to war, and in 1949 he took over the manager's job at Carlisle United. In his day managers were distant and aloof, but Bill was determined to have contact with the people who paid their hard-earned money to support the team – the fans. He used to have a pre-match chat over the Tannoy system, telling the fans what was going on. They loved it.

In 1951 he went to Grimsby Town, then Workington in 1953, ending up at Huddersfield in 1956 where he had a young player called Denis Law. Denis was so talented that Matt Busby wanted to sign him when he was a sixteen-year-old for the then astronomical fee of £10,000, but Denis had just taken apart United's youth team in the FA Youth Cup and Bill too knew a jewel when he saw one. He was having none of it.

In 1959 he became manager of Liverpool. He and Liverpool were made for each other, and they were both transformed as if by magic. Bill completely reorganised the club, beginning with the training facilities, while insisting that the manager had complete control over team selection and transfer policy. He soon had the Liverpool board under his thumb, and appointed former Liverpool player Bob Paisley and Scouser Joe Fagan as his assistants. These three men became the heart of the famous 'boot room' which would run the club for the next 30 years. Bill also changed the team strip to all red (it had been red shirts with white collars, white shorts and hooped

The village of Glenbuck was tiny with a population of about 500, but it spawned 50 professional footballers, eleven of whom played for Scotland.

stockings), saying it made his team look bigger, and he was the one who thought of putting the sign 'This is Anfield' above the players' tunnel just to frighten opponents before they ran out on to the pitch. He developed a great rapport with the players, and the club quickly became his passion. 'There are two famous teams in Liverpool,' he once said, 'Liverpool and Liverpool Reserves.'

Everyone loved Shanks for his eccentricities, even the supporters of other clubs, and stories about him abound. When he went to America he refused to change his watch to American time, saying that British time was the real time. His house backed on to the Everton training ground, and legend had it that he took his dog for a walk on it every night so it would do its odd jobs all over the pitch. Peter Thompson told me once that he was coming in for treatment one Sunday morning when he saw Bill on the pitch with the bus driver in goal, and he was taking penalties against

BELOW LEFT: **Saluting the Anfield faithful at his testimonial, May 1975.**

THE VENABLES VERDICT

• *Had a tough upbringing in a large family in a tiny Scottish miner's cottage.*

• *Completely reorganised and rejuvenated Liverpool on his arrival in 1959. Instigated the great 'boot room' tradition.*

• *A straight-talking, rather eccentric character who enjoyed a terrific rapport with the players and supporters.*

• *Chalked up more than 350 games as a player with Carlisle and Preston. A fiercely competitive wing-half.*

• *As Liverpool manager, led the Merseyside club to three First Division titles, two FA Cups and a UEFA Cup.*

ABOVE: **Holding court in his own inimitable style.**

him. Bill had bet the bus driver he could score ten out of ten. For his eighth penalty, having already scored seven out of seven, Shanks bent down to straighten the ball and proceeded to toe punt it in one movement to try and trick the driver. But the driver caught it. Shanks calmly replaced the ball on the spot saying, 'Seven out of seven.' When the driver protested, the Liverpool manager retorted, 'Don't be stupid, that doesn't count. Do you think I'd take a penalty like that in a match?' When Gordon Williams and I wrote our book *They Used to Play on Grass*, we decided to get quotes for it so we sent it to all the managers, including Shanks. The book had to be set in the future for various reasons, so we had to make a number of prophecies: synthetic pitches, newspapers with colour pictures and the like (a lot of which came true). I was at Liverpool one day and I asked Bill if he had received my book. 'Indeed I have,' he replied, 'and it was fantastic. I think you're the H.G. Wells of football.' I can tell you that he said it with a straight face.

When Bill retired, he never really settled. He still used to turn up at the training ground. When he died of a heart attack in 1981 he left the whole game but particularly Liverpool with so many memories: of the club's great achievements under his management, a host of stories about his wit, wisdom and devotion to duty, and a fund of unforgettable phrases which seemed to flow out of him. They will live on, as will the name and deeds of Bill Shankly.

Alf Ramsey

Single-minded Success

SIR ALF WAS BROUGHT UP NOT FAR FROM THE VENABLES' HOUSE IN DAGENHAM, THOUGH YOU WOULDN'T KNOW IT JUDGING BY OUR ACCENTS. WHEN HE CALLED ME INTO THE ENGLAND SET-UP PRIOR TO THE 1966 WORLD CUP FINALS, MY DAD SAID TO ME, 'TELL HIM I USED TO WORK WITH (SO-AND-SO) DOWN THE DOCKS. HE WAS ALF'S NEXT-DOOR NEIGHBOUR AND HE'LL REMEMBER HIM.'

It sounded reasonable at the time. Now, picture the scene when I turned up for my first senior England squad get-together. For a start, I was in genuine awe of Alf, who came over to me and shook my hand. 'How are you?' he asked. 'Fine, thank you very much,' I replied. 'By the way, my dad says do you remember (so-and-so)? He was your next-door neighbour in Dagenham.' Had I cracked Alf over the head with a baseball bat he couldn't have looked more gobsmacked. He stared at me for what seemed like a long, long time. He didn't utter a single word by way of reply; he simply came out with a sound which if translated into words would probably read something like 'you must be joking'. He must have seen I was embarrassed by this, but he certainly didn't make it easy for me.

But that was Alf. He was aloof, a man who gave very little away until you got to know him as one of his players (I wasn't really around long enough to qualify). But whether you were his type of player or not, there was never any doubt about the feelings of loyalty his England regulars had towards him, the respect they held him in and the regard they had for him as a manager and coach.

He remains the most successful England manager because he is the only one of us who has won the World Cup. On that basis alone Alf has secured his place in the history of our game. And he went on to produce arguably our best team – the one he took to Mexico in 1970. Those finals produced football of a quality we'd never seen before, or since for that matter. The England players competed well with the very best, only going out at the hands of old rivals West Germany after what most would agree was an error of

FACT FILE

FULL NAME: *Sir Alfred Ernest Ramsey*

BORN: *22 January 1920, Dagenham*

DIED: *28 April 1999*

PLAYING CAREER
CLUBS: *Portsmouth (amateur) 1940; Southampton 1943-49; Tottenham Hotspur 1949-55*

APPEARANCES/GOALS:

	League	FA Cup
Southampton	*90/8*	*6/0*
Tottenham Hotspur	*226/24*	*24/0*

CAREER TOTAL: *346 appearances/32 goals*

HONOURS: *First Division Champions 1950-51; First Division runners-up 1951-52; Second Division Champions 1949-50 (all with Tottenham Hotspur)*

INTERNATIONAL: *England 32 appearances/3 goals, 1948-54*

MANAGEMENT CAREER: *Ipswich Town 1955-63; England 1963-74; Birmingham City (caretaker) 1977-78*
HONOURS: *World Cup Winners 1966 (with England); First Division Champions 1961-62; Second Division Champions 1960-61; Third Division (South) Champions 1956-57 (all with Ipswich Town)*

OTHER: *Knighted in January 1967 for services to football; PFA Merit Award 1986 to the England World Cup team; statue erected outside Ipswich Town's Portman Road ground*

OPPOSITE: **Discussing matters with skipper Bobby Moore during England training.**

THE VENABLES VERDICT

- *A single-minded, sometimes awkward character. Not afraid to make enemies.*

- *Played professionally for Southampton and Spurs, winning the First Division title in 1950/51 with the latter. Also won three caps for England.*

- *As manager, took Ipswich Town from the Third Division (South) to the First Division title within the space of five seasons.*

- *Masterminded England's World Cup triumph in 1966.*

- *Knighted in January 1967 for services to football.*

The FA, as usual when dealing with our football icons, treated him less than generously, almost with disdain, if not contempt.

judgement by Alf, an error also highlighted in my piece on Franz Beckenbauer. The game was won, England were going through and Beckenbauer had spent a troubled afternoon in blazing heat tied up by Bobby Charlton. It was then that Alf decided to rest Bobby – a fatal error. The Germans were overjoyed at

Charlton's departure, none more so than the Kaiser who was free to boss the game. But there isn't a single coach who hasn't blundered at one time or another during their career.

The mistake in Mexico was something of a classic, but Alf made fewer mistakes than most. Tactically, he was very astute. He knew what each of his players could give him and he knew what he needed. If that meant leaving out 'names' like Jimmy Greaves, as he did, then he would make that decision. Ron Greenwood at West Ham was recognised as a superb coach,

BELOW: **Getting a point across to the national squad in the run-up to the 1966 World Cup.**

but Alf had the tactical aptitude. Alf reasoned the need for well-coached players and looked to Ron and West Ham to supply them. He used three Hammers: Bobby Moore, Geoff Hurst and Martin Peters. There was to be no requirement for wingers, so the original system of Greaves, Connelly and Paine was replaced by Ball, Peters and Hurst.

I would have liked more time working with him, but from the experiences I did have plus the conversations I've had with his regular players I know he was a charming and knowledgeable man. There seems no doubt about that. He certainly inspired those around him. I contacted him after I was appointed England coach, basically to say hello and show him some respect. In so many ways Alf set the standards to be followed, the most important among which was an insistence on total control of team matters. On that point he did all the tough arguing for those who followed in his footsteps.

But Alf's single-mindedness, some would say downright awkwardness, certainly made him ene-

> **Whether you were his type of player or not, there was never any doubt about the feelings of loyalty his England regulars had towards him.**

mies in the wrong places. Of course England's experiences in the 1970 World Cup weren't enough to dilute the country's debt to him, but the FA, as usual when dealing with our football icons, treated him less than generously, almost with disdain, if not contempt. They apparently had no idea how highly the country thought of Alf. If there had to be a change of manager after we failed to qualify for the next finals in 1974 then Alf's knowledge should still have been retained by the Football Association for the general good of the game. Too many members of the Lancaster Gate club, as they were then (the FA is now based in Soho Square), saw coaches as expendable foot soldiers. Alf was a field marshal to us, but to them – well, England's failure to qualify for the

ABOVE: **Smiling for the camera but Sir Alf was a single-minded and often awkward character.**

1974 finals was the straw the FA were waiting to break his back with. He was sacked and forgotten.

Alf went on to be appointed a director of Birmingham City and even managed them as caretaker for a spell, but it was all a long way from his title success with Ipswich, the World Cup his team won for the country and his subsequent knighthood. What do they say about a prophet never being properly honoured in his own land? Sir Alf would I am sure be contented to know that the people who mattered most to him will always honour his name.

Tom Finney

Modest But Deadly

Bᴵᴸᴸ sʜᴀɴᴋʟʏ ᴊᴜsᴛ ᴀʙᴏᴜᴛ sᴜᴍᴍᴇᴅ ᴜᴘ ᴛᴏᴍ ꜰɪɴɴᴇʏ's ꜰᴏᴏᴛʙᴀʟʟɪɴɢ ᴀʙɪʟɪᴛɪᴇs ᴡʜᴇɴ ʜᴇ sᴀɪᴅ, 'ꜰɪɴɴᴇʏ ᴡᴏᴜʟᴅ ʜᴀᴠᴇ ʙᴇᴇɴ ɢʀᴇᴀᴛ ɪɴ ᴀɴʏ ᴛᴇᴀᴍ, ɪɴ ᴀɴʏ ᴍᴀᴛᴄʜ ᴀɴᴅ ɪɴ ᴀɴʏ ᴀɢᴇ – ᴇᴠᴇɴ ɪꜰ ʜᴇ ʜᴀᴅ ʙᴇᴇɴ ᴡᴇᴀʀɪɴɢ ᴀɴ ᴏᴠᴇʀᴄᴏᴀᴛ.'

And he was an extremely likeable man too, modest despite his extraordinary football skill. He had great respect for his opponents and in return he was respected and admired by everyone he came into contact with. He is one of the few men about whom you can genuinely say it is unlikely he made a single enemy in the game.

Tom Finney was an elegant forward blessed with consummate skill, genuinely two-footed and with strength in the air despite a slight, slim frame. In his early days he played on the right wing where his natural left foot caused massive problems for defenders, who were unsure as to whether he would beat them on the outside or the inside. His pace was deceptive, too. He glided over the turf, always in control.

He was the complete player: outside-left, outside-right and centre-forward. In fact, he was always known as a winger, but he was a wonderful centre-forward. I saw him play in that position for Preston North End against Chelsea, and I think the score was 3-0 to Preston. I was a youth team player then and I'd just come back from a South-East Counties game with Dick Foss. We both watched Finney score all three goals (it might have been four) to win the game. What a display!

The players idolised him. He was known as the 'Preston Plumber', because that was his profession

BELOW: **Leading out Preston North End in November 1959.**

> He is one of the few men about whom you can genuinely say it is unlikely he made a single enemy in the game.

alongside his football career. We were all constantly told that we had to concentrate on being footballers and not do anything else by way of another job. The coaches hated you being distracted by other work; they thought it put you off your game. Divided loyalties were never really a good idea, but Finney just carried on being a plumber.

He was often compared to Sir Stanley Matthews, and some people considered Finney unlucky to be around at the same time as Matthews because Stan

TOM FINNEY
*Preston North End and
England*

FACT FILE

FULL NAME: *Sir Thomas Finney, CBE, OBE, JP*

BORN: *5 April 1922, Preston*

PLAYING CAREER
CLUBS: *Preston North End 1940–60*

APPEARANCES/GOALS:

	League	FA Cup
Preston North End	*433/187*	*40/23*

CAREER TOTAL: *473 appearances/210 goals*

HONOURS: *First Division runners-up 1952–53, 1957–58;
Second Division Champions 1950–51; FA Cup Finalists
1954; Footballer of the Year 1954, 1957*

INTERNATIONAL: *England 76 appearances/30 goals, 1946–59*

OTHER: *President of Preston North End FC; PFA Special
Merit Awards 1979 and 1998*

was the automatic choice on the right wing for England for many years. But Finney would have none of this, considering it an honour to be on the same pitch as the master, let alone in the same team. Finney earned many of his caps playing on the left wing, where he was also world class. Matthews and Finney on either wing was a nightmare scenario for opponents. Just imagine.

> ## He was called into the chairman's office and told that if he didn't play for Preston he wouldn't play for anyone.

Finney was always the great pragmatist, and also an optimist. He would just shrug his shoulders at suggestions that he had been unfortunate in his career and say, 'C'est la vie.'

And there was scope for such suggestions.

Firstly, like many players of his generation,

Finney lost valuable years to the Second World War. His 'official' career was thus effectively limited to 1946 onwards, a fact which denied him the opportunity of maybe another 250 club appearances and 100 goals, plus at least another 40 caps for his country. His first 'full' cap didn't come until September 1946 when the forward line of Finney, Raich Carter, Tommy Lawton, Wilf Mannion and Robert Langton thrashed Northern Ireland 7-2 in Belfast.

Secondly, in 1954 Preston were beaten in the FA Cup final by a last-minute winner from West Bromwich Albion. Everyone remembers the 1953 'Matthews Final' when Stan at last won a medal after twice being denied in the final. Well, in 1954 it seemed as though it would be Finney's turn to cap his career with a winner's medal, but it was not to be. He was, as ever, gracious in defeat.

Thirdly, when an Italian team made it clear to Preston that they wished to buy Finney, he was called into the chairman's office and told that if he didn't play for Preston he wouldn't play for anyone. In those days clubs practically owned players, and Finney lost out on a lot of money as a result. That

LEFT: **An evocative cigarette card from the fifties.**

Italian offer would have been for considerably more than the paltry £14 a week he earned at Preston.

After England's humiliation by Hungary in 1953 when Nandor Hidegkuti demonstrated a new concept in centre-forward play, Finney moved into the centre in a deep-lying position, a role which suited him perfectly. It meant he was in the game more than he had been out on the wing, and by 1957 he had become the first player to win Footballer of the Year twice. He scored 30 goals for his country in twelve years, a record at the time shared by his great friend Nat Lofthouse and broken later by Bobby Charlton, a player whom Finney admired greatly. His last game for England was in 1959 against the USSR at Wembley, England winning 5-0 thanks to a Johnny Haynes hat-trick. Charlton and Lofthouse saw off 'Gentleman Tom' in great style that evening.

His club career came to an end soon after that. Finney played his last League match at Deepdale against Luton Town at the end of the 1959/60 season. A brass band played as both teams and officials linked hands around the centre circle and sang *Auld Lang Syne*.

For many years he has been President of his beloved Preston, his only club. A stand at Deepdale bears his name, his face picked out by coloured seats.

BELOW: **In action for England against Chile in the 1950 World Cup finals.**

Alfredo di Stefano

The Complete Player

THERE IS NO DOUBT ABOUT IT: ALFREDO DI STEFANO WAS EXTRA SPECIAL. I VIVIDLY REMEMBER WATCHING THE 1960 EUROPEAN CUP FINAL ON A BLACK-AND-WHITE TELEVISION SET. THE MATCH WAS PLAYED IN GLASGOW IN FRONT OF A CROWD OF 135,000! REAL MADRID RAN THE GERMAN SIDE EINTRACHT FRANKFURT RAGGED.

It was probably the best game I've ever seen. Can you remember a cup final that finished with a 7-3 score-line? (I know Liverpool's recent UEFA Cup triumph, 5-4 against Alavés, comes close but the European Cup is a much more prestigious competition.)

Alfredo di Stefano was irresistible in that game. For many football experts, he was the world's greatest ever player, despite the claims of Pele and Maradona. However you rank him, it cannot be denied that he was an outstanding footballer.

Nominally a centre-forward, di Stefano possessed phenomenal strength, fitness and energy levels that

> However you rank him, it cannot be denied that he was an outstanding footballer.

enabled him to defend alongside his back four, forage and scheme in midfield, yet also strike with ruthless effectiveness up front. He was the complete footballer in every position. Miguel Munoz, a team-mate of di Stefano's in the all-conquering Real Madrid side of the 1950s, said of the great man, 'With him in your side, you literally had two players in every position.'

Di Stefano's grandfather, originally an Italian from Capri,

emigrated to Argentina. His son turned out for Buenos Aires club River Plate, but just for fun rather than to earn a crust. When, in turn, his sons, Alfredo and Tulio, began to play football with the intention of making it their living, their father was not pleased but he eventually relented. Alfredo made his River

RIGHT: **Di Stefano demonstrates his fantastic ball-juggling abilities, April 1960.**

as they won the Argentinian title in 1947. He also appeared for his country in the South American championships, scoring seven goals in as many matches as Argentina became champions of South America.

In 1949, Argentinian players went on strike as a result of a dispute over pay and conditions. But the clubs refused to give in to the professionals and hired amateurs instead. In Colombia, a country that was outside the jurisdiction of FIFA at this time, a 'pirate' league was set up, attracting players from all over the world. Di Stefano moved to Bogotá's Millonarios club, where Manchester United's Charlie Mitten was also playing.

Since pay and conditions were very good in Bogotá, di Stefano remained there in self-imposed exile. In the early 1950s, FIFA eventually welcomed Colombia back into the fold, and Millonarios embarked on a world tour, playing Real Madrid as part of their fiftieth anniversary celebrations.

Real immediately wanted di Stefano and agreed on a fee with Millonarios on the spot. However, Madrid were unaware that Barcelona had contacted di Stefano's official club, River Plate, and agreed a transfer without the player's knowledge. Now the Spanish Football Association had to decide to which club di Stefano belonged, and a compromise was reached that allowed him to play one season with each team. Barcelona were first but they were generally unimpressed. Di Stefano was sold to Real Madrid. The player was immediately transformed and hit a sensational hat-trick against, yes you've guessed it, Barcelona.

LEFT: **In his civvies on arrival in London with the Spanish national team in October 1960.**

Plate debut on 18 August 1944, aged just 18. He soon acquired the nickname *El Aleman* (the German) on account of his blond hair.

Originally playing on the wing, Alfredo was loaned to Huracan to complete his football education, returning to his parent club as a centre-forward. Di Stefano quickly became one of River Plate's stars

With di Stefano in the side, things started happening in Madrid. Real won the Spanish League twice in 1954 and 1955, the latter success qualifying them for the inaugural European Cup in 1956. Madrid were now fielding an all-star side drawn from many different countries, with di Stefano the pivotal figure around which everything flowed. Amazingly, the Spanish club won the first five European Cups, beating Reims 4-3 in 1956, Fiorentina 2-0 in 1957, AC Milan 3-2 (after extra time) in 1958, Reims (again) 2-0 in 1959 and then, of course, Eintracht Frankfurt 7-3 in 1960. Alfredo di Stefano scored in every one of these finals, including the hat-trick in Glasgow that I will always remember.

The great man was highly instrumental in Real Madrid adding six more Spanish League titles (1957, 1958, 1961, 1962, 1963 and 1964), a Spanish Cup (1962) and a World Club Championship (1960). What a stunning catalogue of success!

After his playing career had come to an end with Espanyol, di Stefano embarked on a managerial career that took in spells at Boca Juniors, Valencia and Real Madrid. I recall meeting him when I was manager of Barcelona and he was manager of Real Madrid. Our teams had played each other and I think Barcelona won 3-0. I have to say that I was over-awed when

BELOW: **Looking the part in the all-white of Real Madrid in 1963.**

FACT FILE

FULL NAME: *Alfredo di Stefano*

BORN: *4 July 1926, Barracas, Buenos Aires*

PLAYING CAREER

CLUBS: *River Plate (Argentina) 1944–49; Huracan (Argentina) (loan 1947); Millonarios (Colombia) 1949–53; Real Madrid 1953–64; Espanyol 1964*

APPEARANCES/GOALS: *accurate records are not available; di Stefano scored 218 goals in 228 League matches for Real Madrid; 377 in all matches including a record 49 in the Champions Cup; in Colombia he scored over 200 goals; his overall career total is at least 790 goals (possibly 873) in over 800 matches (the fourth in the all-time list headed by Pelé, and the highest for a midfield player).*

HONOURS: *European Cup Winners 1956, 1957, 1958, 1959, 1960; World Club Champions 1960; Spanish League Champions 1954, 1955, 1957, 1958, 1961, 1962, 1963, 1964; Spanish Cup Winners 1962 (all with Real Madrid); Argentinian League Champions 1947 (with River Plate)*

INTERNATIONAL: *Argentina 7 appearances/7 goals, 1947; Colombia, not known; Spain 31 appearances/23 goals, 1957–61*

HONOURS: *South American Champions 1947 (with Argentina)*

MANAGEMENT CAREER

CLUBS: *Boca Juniors 1968–70; Valencia 1970–82; Real Madrid 1982–83, 1990*

HONOURS: *Spanish League Championship 1971 (with Valencia)*

I came face-to-face with the great man. I just couldn't believe I was meeting one of my idols. And here I was, an opposing manager. It was one of those situations that you just cannot imagine ever happening, even in your wildest dreams.

Di Stefano was one of the very few players to play international football for three different countries. He had already played for his native Argentina when, in 1947, his move to Colombia made him *persona non grata*. He was capped by Colombia and when he became a naturalised Spaniard in 1957, he eventually played 31 times for his adopted country, scoring 23 goals. Quite a strike rate! Unfortunately for di

> Di Stefano was charming and easy to talk to, a gentleman on and off the pitch, a genius to all those who had the pleasure of watching him play.

Stefano, despite Real Madrid's domination of European club football, the national side could not match the club's achievements on the international stage. So di Stefano, like George Best, was destined never to display his talents at the greatest show of them all, the World Cup finals. Football fans around the world were denied that particular privilege.

THE VENABLES VERDICT

- To my mind, the game's most complete player – equally comfortable defending, pulling the strings in midfield or scoring goals.

- Captivated a huge television audience with a hat-trick in Real Madrid's breathtaking 7-3 demolition of Eintracht Frankfurt in the 1960 European Cup final.

- Was instrumental in Real Madrid's five consecutive European Cup triumphs from 1956 to 1960, scoring in each and every final.

- Internationally, played for Argentina, Colombia and Spain. Never made a World Cup finals.

- An unpretentious man. Gentlemanly and charming.

Di Stefano would weave his magic in every area of the pitch – at the back, up front, in the middle – and still score goals. He could defend, pull the strings in midfield, then press forward to get his name on the scoresheet. Pele and Maradona are certainly two of the greatest ever players, but to my mind di Stefano was definitely the most complete player. 'The white arrow', as he was known in Spain, was also a very normal man, not at all pretentious. He was charming and easy to talk to, a gentleman on and off the pitch, a genius to all those who had the pleasure of watching him play. A master craftsman at work.

BELOW: **Wembley holds its breath as the great man fires in a shot on goal for Spain.**

Johnny Brooks

A Real Hometown Boy

JOHNNY BROOKS WAS THE COMPLETE OPPOSITE OF JIMMY HILL IN THE SENSE THAT HIS CONFIDENCE WAS VERY FRAGILE. HE WAS A BRILLIANTLY GIFTED INSIDE-FORWARD WHOSE ABILITY AMAZED ME. WHEN JOHNNY WAS 'ON HIS GAME' HE GLIDED AROUND THE PITCH OOZING CLASS AND PROVIDING ME WITH WONDERFUL MEMORIES.

His ball control was exceptional – he had the rare ability to run faster with the ball than without it. Johnny could also pass the ball wonderful well, both long and short. He had an unforgettable body swerve that enabled him to change direction at acute angles that would not only make defenders lose balance, but also make supporters fall out of their seats.

> He hated the pressure of the professional game. All he wanted to do was just play football for fun like we all did as kids in the park.

Johnny played at Spurs between 1953 and 1959. Then he came to Chelsea in December 1959 in exchange for Les Allen. This is where I came into contact with him. He was my hero because he had such natural skills, was beautifully balanced and built like an Adonis. I remember the three internationals he played in – against Denmark, Wales and Yugoslavia – and he should have won many more caps because he was such a great player. However, Johnny Haynes was the automatic choice for England in that position.

When I played my first game for Chelsea against West Ham at 17, Johnny was in the Chelsea team. It was my debut but he was the one who was nervous! It was unbelievable. I was playing in a League game with my hero so it was a big moment for me. We went in at half-time one-nil up and I was sitting opposite Johnny in the dressing-room. He stood up, mug of tea in hand, strolled over in that impressive style of his, sat down next to me and I thought this was it – words of advice or encouragement, some gold dust from my idol. Instead, he turned round to me and asked, 'How do you think I'm doing?' I was dumbfounded. A legend who has played 500 games asking a kid of 17 how he is doing. I was flabbergasted and rolled over with laughter.

John was always negative when speaking about the opposition and the likelihood of us winning the next game. I was the reverse.

He was unable to recapture his early form with Spurs and less than two seasons later – in September

FACT FILE

FULL NAME: *John Brooks*

BORN: *23 December 1931, Reading*

PLAYING CAREER
CLUBS: *Reading 1949–53; Tottenham Hotspur 1953–59; Chelsea 1959–61; Brentford 1961–63; Crystal Palace 1964; Toronto (Canadian League) 1965*

APPEARANCES/GOALS:

	League	FA Cup	FL Cup
Reading	46/5	3/1	
Tottenham Hotspur	166/46	13/5	
Chelsea	46/6	2/0	4/1
Brentford	83/36	7/1	3/0
Crystal Palace	7/0		

CAREER TOTAL: *380 appearances/101 goals*

HONOURS: *Fourth Division Champions 1962–63 (Brentford)*

INTERNATIONAL: *England 3 appearances/2 goals, 1956*

1961 – he was on the move again, this time to Brentford for a fee of £3,000. He played 83 League matches and scored 36 goals for the club in two seasons. During this time Brentford enjoyed their biggest ever League win, 9-0 over Wrexham at Griffin Park, a game in which Brooks scored twice. Johnny won his one and only medal with Brentford, the Fourth Division championship in 1962/63. What a very modest reward for such a great player.

In spite of his immense insecurities and lack of confidence, Johnny is remembered with much affection by all the clubs he played for. He was born in Reading and was the first player from the Berkshire town to play for England. When he was a young man in the Reading first team, he is remembered by young contemporaries as enjoying a kick about in the local park. If Johnny was passing by the park on his way home from training, he would always join in with the local lads, despite the fact that we was wearing his smart clothes. He would invariably complain that he had ruined his winkle-pickers, but he was probably happiest when he was just kicking a ball around in the local park.

In some ways his talent was a burden to him. He hated the pressure of the professional game. All he wanted to do was just play football for fun like we all did as kids in the park. Maybe he was right. He didn't want to have to perform or for people to criticise or analyse his displays. It was fortunate that he played when he did because he would have hated the media attention and all the pressure that goes with being a top-class sportsman in the modern era.

Today, at nearly 70, he is still very fit and turns out in benefit, testimonial and charity matches. He played in Reading's final match at Elm Park in September 1998 in a veterans' tournament.

At Spurs I started a 'Legends' club (ex-players would be invited to games and made to feel very welcome) because I realised that many supporters still wanted to talk to the old players who were still around. In Barcelona and Italy veterans are revered, but here they are almost forgotten and I think that's wrong. A great many fans still remember the old

players and want to have the chance to meet and chat to them. Johnny Brooks was a part of the Legends club and kept it going and Dave Webb – who was then manager at Chelsea – did the same at Stamford Bridge and it took off all over the country.

Funnily enough, Johnny's son Sean became an England schoolboy international and played a total of 381 League matches in his career, just one more than his dad. Sean also scored 45 goals as a midfield player for Crystal Palace. Guess who signed him for Palace? I did. He was a very talented youngster and I didn't at first realise that he was the legendary

> **Johnny was my hero because he had such natural skills, was beautifully balanced and built like an Adonis.**

Johnny Brooks' boy. Like father like son.

Johnny now lives in Bournemouth, but he still likes to get up to Reading's Madejski Stadium to see his hometown club play. He is a Reading boy through and through and I don't think much will keep him away from watching his first club. He is one of those men who will always remain loyal to his roots and I have tremendous respect for that.

There was a wonderfully mischievous side to Johnny's character when his tail was up. In training he had a trick where he would get close to a defender then stoop and grab his knee in mock agony. The defender would become distracted and would show concern about the 'injury', just as Johnny was skipping away with the ball. (He even did it in a game once I remember!) Then there was a golf match at

I thought this was it – words of advice, some gold dust from my idol. Instead, he turned round to me and asked, 'How do you think I'm doing?'

Broadstairs in which I joined Johnny, Tony Nicholas and Ron Tindall for a foursome. Tony and Ron were striding out in front and Johnny had found himself in a bunker. He had forgotten about little old me, who was thrashing about horribly and bringing up the rear. What Johnny didn't realise was that I saw him have three or four unsuccessful swipes from the bunker. Then he threw the ball out with his left hand, along with a handful of sand with his right. I had caught him red-handed! He had a big smirk on his face.

The vision of Johnny going past defenders effortlessly with that magnificent body swerve gives me a great thrill and wonderful memories. He is a star that shone so brightly for me, in spite of his frailties.

BELOW: **The Chelsea team of 1960. Johnny is on the far left of the front row. I'm next to him.**

John Charles

The Gentle Giant

I VIVIDLY REMEMBER STANDING ALONGSIDE JOHN CHARLES WHEN I WAS JUST 18 AND PLAYING FOR CHELSEA. HE WAS AWE-INSPIRING, LIKE DUNCAN EDWARDS. BUILT LIKE A BRICK WAREHOUSE, JOHN WAS KNOWN AS 'THE GENTLE GIANT' AND IN ITALY AS *IL BUON GIGANTE*. AT HIS PEAK HE WAS 6 FEET 2 INCHES TALL AND WEIGHED 14 STONE. HE WAS A GOD.

John has gone down as the greatest player that Wales has ever produced. He was also one of the few British players to have been judged a great success in Italian football. He grew up in Swansea in South Wales in the thirties and forties but joined Leeds United as a junior in 1947 before signing professional terms in January 1949.

In spite of his size, Charles was essentially a skilful player with a delicate touch and a tremendous shot in both feet. His height gave him dominance in the air and – as you would expect – he was a powerful header of the ball. John was a remarkable player in many ways, not least for his versatility. He could play at centre-forward or centre-half with equal ease, indeed he played centre-forward for Juventus and centre-half for his country. He was top class in both positions.

Despite John's considerable talents, Leeds United were a poor side during his first period with the club,

> **Juventus paid Leeds £70,000 for Charles' services, which was more than double the British record.**

stuck in the old Second Division between 1947 and 1956. It would take the arrival of Don Revie in 1961 to elevate Leeds to the top level.

In the 1953/54 season, John scored 42 League goals in the Second Division – still a club record to this day. Despite this remarkable achievement, Leeds could finish only tenth in the table. Two seasons

later, United finished second to Sheffield Wednesday and returned to the First Division after a gap of nine seasons. This promotion was Charles' only honour with the club.

After one season back in the top flight, the football world was taken aback when Turin's Juventus paid Leeds £70,000 for Charles' services, which was more than double the British record. At this stage John was receiving about £14 a week in the English game. Juventus paid him a £10,000 signing-on fee, plus £60 per week basic wages with fringe benefits.

FACT FILE

FULL NAME: *William John Charles CBE*

BORN: *27 December 1931, Swansea*

PLAYING CAREER

CLUBS: *Leeds United 1949–57, 1962; Juventus 1957–62; AS Roma 1962–63; Cardiff City 1963–66*

APPEARANCES/GOALS:

	League	FA Cup	FL Cup	European
Leeds United	308/153	19/4		
Juventus	155/93			
AS Roma	*not available*			
Cardiff City	65(1)/19	1/0	2/0	5/0

CAREER TOTAL: *551(1) appearances/269 goals*

HONOURS: *Second Division runners-up (promoted) 1955–56 (with Leeds United); Italian League Champions 1958, 1960, 1961; Italian Cup Winners 1959, 1960 (all with Juventus); awarded the CBE, 2001*

INTERNATIONAL: *Wales 38 appearances/15 goals, 1950–65*

MANAGEMENT CAREER: *non-league clubs*

John was a fantastic success in Italy. The fans took him to their hearts and he is revered in Turin today. His presence galvanised both the club and its supporters. He helped Juve win the Italian League title three times (1957/58, 1959/60 and 1960/1961) and the Italian Cup twice (1959 and 1960). In all, John scored 93 goals in 155 matches – an extraordinary ratio in the highly defensive Italian game.

LEFT: **John's physical presence gave him dominance in the air.**

OPPOSITE: **Another goal with his head, this time against Milan's Internazionale.**

Unlike other British players such as Jimmy Greaves, Denis Law and Joe Baker who didn't enjoy their times in Italy, John Charles settled quickly and easily. He learned the language, enjoyed the lifestyle, fully accepted the Italian way of life in his quiet, urbane fashion. He was wise when he said:

Playing in Italy is just like going into one of the Services. If you try to kick against everything then you are in for a miserable time. If you take the attitude that you are in, and you might as well enjoy yourself, in spite of the rules and regulations, then the chances are you won't have such a bad time. You must tell yourself you are getting well paid, and put up with strictness and soul-destroying defensive football. Then you will have a fine time.

John played one game for Juventus as a centre-half, against their great city rivals Torino. He always used his elbows to full advantage when challenging for the ball but on this occasion he inadvertently caught an opponent on the chin and knocked him out. Seeing the player on the ground, John kicked the ball into touch. Everyone in the stadium was stunned into silence. Juventus won the game 1-0 and later John heard a terrific commotion outside his apartment. As he emerged through the front door to

> John learned the language, enjoyed the lifestyle, fully accepted the Italian way of life in his quiet, urbane fashion.

investigate, he was greeted by a crowd of Torino supporters who clapped him furiously and slapped him on the back. They wanted to applaud the sportsmanship of *Il Buon Gigante*. John invited them in for a drink.

He once incurred the wrath of the team owner, Signor Agnelli, who also happened to own the Fiat car company. John had a liking for Citroën cars and once Agnelli found out he telephoned his star player immediately. 'What do you think you are doing? You're driving a Citroën? A French car? Don't you know that I own Fiat? Get rid of the Citroën at once. I'll have a Fiat delivered first thing in the morning.' There was no arguing with Signor Agnelli!

John made his international debut for Wales in March 1950 at the age of just 18. He played at centre-half against Northern Ireland at Wrexham. His brother Mel was

BELOW: **Taking to the field for Juventus against Arsenal at Highbury in November 1958.**

• *Charles was 6 feet 2 inches tall and weighed 14 stone. He was built like a brick warehouse.*

• *Strong in the air, but also possessed a delicate touch and tremendous shooting prowess.*

• *British fans dubbed him 'The Gentle Giant', Italian supporters Il Buon Gigante.*

• *Helped Juventus to win three Italian League titles, in 1957/58, 1959/60 and 1960/1961.*

• *Had a remarkable scoring record in the highly defensive Italian game – 93 goals in just 155 matches.*

• *Won 38 Welsh caps in a 15-year international career.*

also a fine footballer who played for Arsenal and was capped 31 times for Wales, often alongside big brother John. In 1955 the brothers Charles and the brothers Allchurch (Ivor and Len) all turned out against Northern Ireland. The Welsh won 3–2 and John helped himself to a hat-trick.

Charles led his native Wales to their first ever World Cup finals in 1958, in Sweden. Against the odds, Wales got through their group stage against Hungary, Mexico and hosts Sweden (who topped the group), before losing to the eventual winners Brazil 1-0 to a late Pele goal after a hugely brave defensive display. In a 15-year international career, John won 38 caps for his country and scored 15 goals.

Four years later, Charles decided to return to England, Don Revie signing him for Leeds for a massive £53,000 as the 1962/63 season began. But after just 11 matches Charles discovered he just couldn't settle back home, and he wanted to return to Italy. AS Roma snapped him up for £65,000, which was a quick and tidy profit for Leeds. But this time in Italy he only stayed one season and returned to South Wales and Cardiff City, where he played another 74 games and scored another 19 goals before retiring in 1966.

TOP RIGHT: **Doing up his laces in the changing room, January 1963.**

John Charles can be very proud of the fact that despite

In the 1953/54 season, John scored 42 League goals for Leeds United in the Second Division – still a club record to this day. Despite this remarkable achievement, Leeds could finish only tenth in the table.

playing in the world's toughest leagues, he was never sent off and never even cautioned. That tells you a great deal about his wonderful sense of sportsmanship and fair play. In 1972 he turned out alongside Hungarian legend Ferenc Puskas in an 'old boys' international at Stamford Bridge for Europe against Great Britain. Charles scored three and Puskas one in a 5-4 win for Europe. A fitting tribute to a legend.

Johnny Haynes

The Level-headed Maestro

To my mind, Johnny Haynes can take his place amongst England's greatest players. He was a wonderfully gifted inside-forward, foraging deep to pick up the ball in midfield, a master of the weighted pass, whether short or long.

To complete his many skills, Haynes could score more than his share of goals, although by no stretch of the imagination could he be considered an out-and-out goalscorer.

He is regarded as the finest passer of a ball in the history of English football. His ability to find gaps in the opposition defence, at any level of the game, marked him out as one of the sport's great players, despite his lack of basic pace.

Even though it was traditional for a player to spend his career with one club, it is still remarkable that a player as gifted as Johnny Haynes should spend his entire football career with Fulham – a club that traditionally struggled to compete at the top level. This didn't really have any bearing on his international career since he was first choice for England for seven years.

I think Johnny highlights the difference between that era of the fifties and sixties compared to today when players fall over themselves to join the clubs that pay the highest salaries and that are more likely

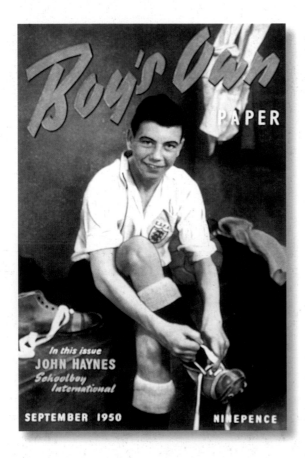

> I believe that Johnny was one of the best players this country has produced, and the finest passer of the ball.

to win trophies. Johnny Haynes was headhunted by AC Milan, but nothing came of it. Apart from anything else, clubs had a much stronger hold over players in those days.

Despite Fulham's modest status in the English game, Haynes was still the first £100-a-week player following the lifting of the maximum wage in the early sixties. The bigger clubs paid nothing like this to their best players. He was also the Brylcreem Boy. There was a man called Bagnell Harvey who was one of the first agents to get players involved in advertising and promoting products in this way. I guess it was the forerunner of the huge sponsorship contracts that the players enjoy today.

Johnny's ability to find gaps in the opposition defence, at any level of the game, marked him out as one of the sport's great players.

Having signed as a professional player for Fulham in 1952, Johnny would play 657 first class games for his one club without winning any honours. Fulham had just dropped into the Second Division after a brief three-year stay in the top flight. It would be 1959 before Fulham and Haynes would return to the First Division.

Johnny missed nearly all of the 1962/63 season due to a horrific car crash in Blackpool. He was seri-

ously injured and this effectively ended his international career. The crash had a serious effect on Haynes' health for the rest of his playing days.

The nearest Johnny came to winning a major trophy with Fulham came in 1958 when the West London team reached the FA Cup semi-final, where they met a Manchester United side still coming to terms with the Munich air disaster. United's patched-up team drew with Fulham at Villa Park before going on to Wembley after an exciting 5-3 win at Highbury in the replay.

After the sacking of Bobby Robson in 1968, Johnny briefly became Fulham's player/manager, with Bill Dodgin as his assistant. Dodgin took over the management chair the following season.

Johnny made his England debut in November 1955 against Northern Ireland at Wembley, alongside the legendary Tom Finney. England won 3-0. His first international goal was scored at Hampden Park in April 1956 and earned England a 1-1 draw. I watched him play for his country more than once, including games against Scotland and Mexico, which England won 9-3 and 8-0 respectively. He imposed his authority on both games. I always wanted to play like him. I was a similar player in the sense that I liked to pass the ball, but he was just much, much better at it!

I remember Johnny contributing to a momentous England game at Wembley in 1956 against the emerging Brazil side. It was one of Stanley Matthews' last international appearances. It was a case of England's oldest player alongside England's youngest, Duncan Edwards. Johnny Haynes starred in a remarkable match that England won 4-2.

Johnny also played in Stanley Matthews' last ever England appearance in Copenhagen in May 1957. He scored in a 4-1 win.

He appeared in both the 1958 and 1962 World Cup finals in Sweden and Chile respectively. England achieved little in either of the tournaments, but this didn't damage Johnny's reputation. This was quite an

TOP LEFT: **Exchanging pennants with his Austrian counterpart at Wembley, April 1962.**

THE VENABLES VERDICT

● *A deep-foraging inside-forward who was a master of the weighted pass.*

● *Always level-headed. Didn't let external factors affect his game.*

● *Was the fulcrum of the England side at the 1962 World Cup finals in Chile. England disappointed but Haynes' reputation was enhanced.*

● *Won 56 caps for his country, scoring 18 goals. Skippered England 22 times.*

● *Was a loyal servant of Fulham for nearly two decades before emigrating to South Africa.*

achievement because often when the national side plays badly all the players are tarred with the same brush. But Johnny always stood head-and-shoulders above the rest in so many respects.

Johnny was a key figure in England's most prolific spell in the modern era. Between October 1960 and May 1961 they beat Northern Ireland 5-2, Luxembourg 9-0, Spain 4-2, Wales 5-1, Scotland 9-3 and Mexico 8-0. Haynes and Bobby Robson formed a wonderfully creative midfield that allowed Jimmy Greaves, Bobby Smith and Bobby Charlton to run riot.

BELOW: **Johnny demonstrates his recovery from a broken leg before Fulham's FA Cup tie with West Ham United, January 1963.**

His international career came to a close at the 1962 World Cup finals in Chile. England went out in the quarter-finals to Brazil, losing 3-1 to the eventual champions. Garrincha was just too good for the England defence. At this stage, England were relying too heavily on Johnny, their captain – the entire team strategy depended on exploiting Haynes' great skills to the full. This rather one-dimensional approach was not lost on opposing coaches, who took steps to ensure Johnny was closely marked throughout, reducing

BELOW: **With new Fulham manager Vic Buckingham (far left) and Josh Chamberlain, Maurice Cook and Joe Bacuzzi in the dressing room at Craven Cottage.**

> **I always wanted to play like Johnny. I was a similar player in the sense that I liked to pass the ball, but he was just much, much better at it!**

England's effectiveness considerably.

By 1966 Johnny's England career was over, so he missed England's biggest ever football party. I very much doubt whether Johnny would have fitted into Alf Ramsey's set-up. Ramsey wanted team players rather than exceptionally gifted individuals, which is

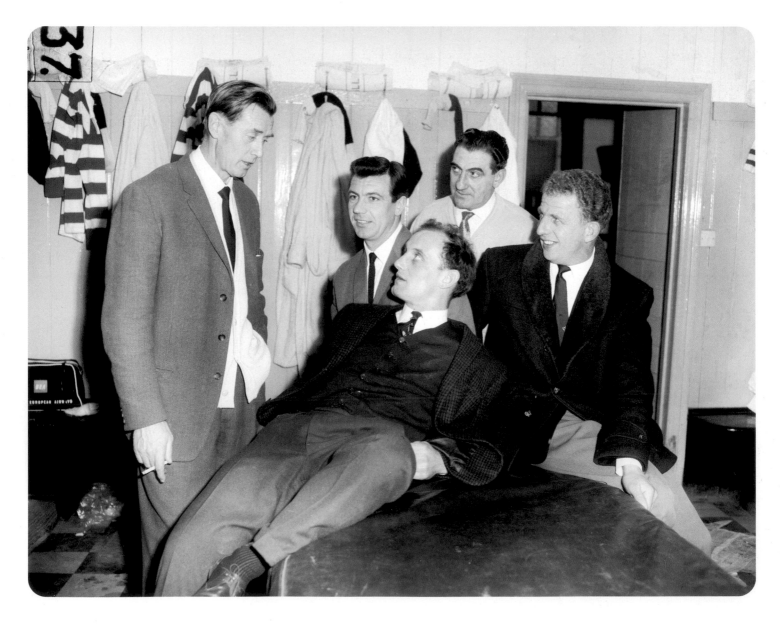

why Jimmy Greaves was virtually redundant.

In 1970, with his Fulham career over, Johnny emigrated to South Africa. He joined Durban City, and led them to a league championship, his only trophy. At the same time, his beloved Fulham were struggling, enduring two consecutive relegations and ending up in the Third Division for the first time since 1932.

I believe that Johnny was one of the best players this country has produced. He was also a very steady person, which helped him keep a straight-line approach to life – that's vitally important. When a player finds himself in the public eye, his ups and downs are magnified ten-fold and it's so important not to get too up when it goes well or too down when it goes badly. Johnny was one of those people who just kept going and kept doing what he did best without allowing external factors to affect him.

ABOVE: **Feeling the full force of a Nobby Stiles challenge in March 1967.**

Johnny was the Brylcreem Boy. I guess it was the forerunner of the huge advertising contracts the players enjoy today.

FACT FILE

FULL NAME: *John Norman Haynes*

BORN: *17 October 1934, Edmonton*

PLAYING CAREER
CLUBS: *Fulham 1952–70; Durban City (South Africa)*

APPEARANCES/GOALS: *Fulham, League 594/146, FA Cup 43/9, FL Cup 20/2*

CAREER TOTAL: *657 appearances/157 goals*

HONOURS: *Second Division runners-up (promoted) 1958–59; won a SA Championship medal with Durban City (not first class)*

INTERNATIONAL: *England 56 appearances/18 goals, 1955–62; captain on 22 occasions*

Duncan Edwards

Cut Short in his Prime

FEBRUARY 6 1958 WILL BE FOREVER LINKED TO ONE OF THE MOST TRAGIC EVENTS IN FOOTBALL. THE MUNICH AIR CRASH TOOK THE LIVES OF SO MANY YOUNG BUDDING FOOTBALL STARS. IT IS ONE OF THOSE DAYS WHEN EVERYONE REMEMBERS WHERE THEY WERE AND WHAT THEY WERE DOING WHEN THEY HEARD THE FATEFUL NEWS.

I was standing at St Martin's Corner in Dagenham waiting for a bus to take me to training at West Ham. The story was up on the newspaper billboards: 'AIR CRASH. FOOTBALLERS IN AIR CRASH'. I just couldn't believe it. All these young men in the prime of their life – players you thought of as immortal – were dead, and others were seriously injured. There was a daily bulletin about the injured, speculating about whether they were likely to survive or not. I would wake every morning and Duncan was the first thing on my mind. I would dash to buy a newspaper to find out the latest state of his health.

Duncan Edwards was my hero. I had seen him play for Manchester United against Arsenal on 1 February. United won 5-4 in the battle to win their third consecutive championship title. It was Duncan

Edwards' finest League match. And here he was fighting for his life in hospital.

Duncan was incredibly strong. He was 5 feet 11 inches tall and weighed 13 stone. He was described as a 'manboy'. His position was half-back. Blessed with all the football attributes – size, speed, control, power and unlimited courage – he also had the most delicate of touches when necessary. Duncan combined raw power and sublime subtlety.

Edwards was an undoubted star, burning brightly before being cruelly snatched away. In the crash he had suffered horrendous injuries, and battled for two weeks before finally succumbing. Had he not been so strong, he would have almost certainly died in the crash. I cried when the news of his death broke.

He first played for England at the age of 18 and died at 21. He scored five goals at international level, unbelievable for a half-back. I think he would have been one of the greatest players of all time.

I can remember hearing a particular story about him. He was playing for the Manchester United youth team against Chelsea. It was the FA Youth Cup and the game was being badly affected by gale-force winds. Duncan was positioned at centre-forward and, playing with the benefit of the wind, scored two goals to give United a 2-0 lead at the interval. During the half-time break it was decided that Duncan would switch to centre-half because United wanted to keep Chelsea out against the wind. The boy did it on his own. He

LEFT: **Another all-action display from Duncan: England versus Spain, Madrid, May 1955.**

Imagine a player who can play centre-half like Jaap Stam, full-back like Paolo Maldini, midfield like Roy Keane and centre-forward like Alan Shearer.

was incredible, a remarkable player for one so young. He was capable of playing brilliantly in any position on the field. Imagine a player who can play centre-half like Jaap Stam, full-back like Paolo Maldini, midfield like Roy Keane and centre-forward like Alan Shearer.

In Febuary 1955 the England Under-23 team played their Scottish counterparts, with Duncan Edwards at left-half. Halfway through the first half, England lost their centre-forward through injury.

Substitutes were only just being introduced in international football at this time, but only one per team was permitted. England's substitute was a half-back so Edwards was moved to centre-forward and within fifteen minutes he had scored three times. England went on to thrash the Scots 6-0.

Just over a couple of years later, Manchester United visited AFC Bournemouth in the sixth round of the FA Cup, the home side having just disposed of Tottenham Hotspur in the previous round. United's regular centre-forward, Tommy Taylor, was absent injured and was replaced by the versatile Edwards. Within a quarter of an hour, United centre-half Mark Jones was carried off badly injured. There were no substitutes at this time, so Edwards moved to centre-half and

United's ten men came back from 1-0 down at half-time to win 2-1. Edwards' tremendous display at centre-half was pivotal in United's win, and kept their Treble hopes alive.

The previous year England had met West Germany in Berlin. Edwards scored his first international goal with a spectacular shot from 25 yards to give his side the lead. England won 3-1 and the Germans christened Edwards 'Boom boom' for his shooting power. You have to understand just how gigantic the man was in footballing terms, and how much of a loss his death was to football, both nationally and internationally.

The day before the tragic crash, United had played their European Cup second leg quarter-final tie in Belgrade. United had gained a 3-0 half-time advantage to establish a 5-1 aggregate lead. Red Star fought back – aided by some eccentric refereeing – and scored in the last second of the match to retain some pride and secure a 3-3 draw on the day. But United and Edwards were through.

ABOVE RIGHT: **A bubble gum collector's card from 1957.**

RIGHT: **Edwards wearing his England Schoolboys cap in 1951.**

Then to that last fateful day. On 6 February 1958, the plane carrying the United players stopped to refuel in Munich. The plane attempted to take off in treacherously snowy conditions and crashed into a building at the end of the runway. At a stroke there ended an era.

Duncan was born in Dudley in the West Midlands and his death affected the city greatly. One of their favourite sons had been taken and there was a huge sense of shock and disbelief.

Some strange coincidences

FACT FILE

FULL NAME: *Duncan Edwards*

BORN: *1 October 1936, Dudley, West Midlands*

DIED: *21 February 1958*

PLAYING CAREER
CLUBS: *Manchester United 1952–58*

APPEARANCES/GOALS: *Manchester United, League 151/20, FA Cup 12/1, European 12/0*

CAREER TOTAL: *175 appearances/21 goals*

HONOURS: *First Division Champions 1955–56, 1956–57; FA Cup Finalist 1956–57; European Cup Semi-final 1956–57; FA Youth Cup Winner 1952–53, 1953–54, 1954–55 (all with Manchester United)*

INTERNATIONAL: *England 18 appearances/5 goals, 1955-58; youngest ever English international at 18 years 183 days, beaten since by Michael Owen; England U-23 6 appearances/5 goals, 1954-57*

have happened to link my life with Duncan Edwards. For a start, my mum was going to call me Duncan. She always wanted me to be called that but my aunt Mary used to tell her that it was a terrible name. The two of them would argue. One day, as my Aunt Mary was leaving the house, she nodded her head and said, 'See you Eileen. See you Dunc.' Of course, that put my mum off immediately, so Terry it was.

I was delighted to be awarded an honorary degree from the University of Wolverhampton a few years ago. When I went to attend the ceremony I discovered that the university was actually in Dudley. For years, whenever United played Wolves at Molineux, United fans would lay flowers on Duncan's grave. There is also a stained glass window in the parish church of St Francis in Dudley that shows Duncan in his playing kit (see photo, left).

When he died, it was very hard for Duncan's parents. His dad took

BELOW: **Duncan (far right) awaits his turn to meet Lord Roseberry before the 1957 England/Scotland clash.**

> I was in Dagenham waiting for a bus to take me to training at West Ham. The story was up on the newspaper billboards: 'AIR CRASH. FOOTBALLERS IN AIR CRASH'. I just couldn't believe it.

a job in the local cemetery where his beloved son is buried, and personally tended his grave on a daily basis. I think very few people within football escaped from the shock waves of the death of the Busby Babes.

I believe life does have strange coincidences. Things happen, or things are said, or people meet at certain times, that often have great significance. I remember when my own dad died I was with Crystal Palace in Durham for a game against Sunderland. We went up with the team the previous day and the next morning, before the game, my wife Toots rang to say my dad had died from a heart attack. I immediately got on a train from Durham to London. Then years later I took the job at Middlesbrough. I lived in Darlington, close to Durham, and the first game I had in charge was against Sunderland. It was strange thinking of all the clubs we could have played against. It was almost as though there was unfinished business. How can you explain it any other way?

In Duncan Edwards' case, I simply think it was very sad that we were all unable to enjoy watching his talents develop further. The loss of all the Busby Babes has somehow left its sad legacy in football. Manchester United were famous before that – and after the crash they became one of the most famous clubs in the world, and they have been phenomenally successful – but that crash was the end of an era. It could also be argued that from the most tragic of circumstances Manchester United developed as a world sporting power. I don't think you can fail to be affected by these momentous world events.

TOP RIGHT: **April 1957 and flourishing as one of Busby's Babes. Ten months later, he was dead.**

THE VENABLES VERDICT

- *Edwards had size, speed, control, delicacy, power and unlimited courage – he combined raw power and sublime subtlety.*

- *Incredible versatility. Just as comfortable at centre-forward as at half-back or centre-half.*

- *First capped for England at just 18. Scored five goals from the half-back position.*

- *Aged 21, tragically killed in the Munich air crash, along with many other Busby Babes.*

- *His early death was a huge loss to the football community, both nationally and internationally.*

Bobby Charlton

A National Treasure

THERE ISN'T A COUNTRY IN THE WORLD WHERE I'VE NOT HEARD THE NAME BOBBY CHARLTON. IT CAN BE A REMOTE PART OF JAPAN OR SOME MARKET IN SOUTH AMERICA, BUT AS SOON AS YOU CALL A CAB, SIT IN A RESTAURANT, BUY A COFFEE OR JUST HAVE A REST, SOMEONE WILL SAY: 'ENGLISH? BOBBY CHARLTON!' QUITE OFTEN THESE ARE THE ONLY ENGLISH WORDS THEY KNOW, EVEN IF THEY DON'T REALLY KNOW HOW TO PRONOUNCE THEM PROPERLY.

They have seen him on TV or on some video or other, they have watched him score one of those hallmark goals of his, they have been impressed by him, they remember the strands of hair trailing behind him as he finishes a long run with a thundering shot, and they remember that powerful physique. He is instantly recognisable, probably the most recognisable Englishman after the Prime Minister, though I suspect Bobby would be more popular worldwide.

His celebrity is truly astonishing. How one person, and not the most glamorous of figures either, has made such an impression in places from Bombay to Buenos Aires, from London to Sydney and lots of places we've never heard of in between is testimony to the respect he has earned for his brilliance and sheer honesty as a player, for his skills on the field and his down-to-earth attitude. He has been our footballing ambassador for a number of years now and no one could do it better or with more enthusiasm. His name is a byword for Englishness. He has extended his career from being a high-profile player with England and Manchester United to being an equally high-profile traveller, globetrotting on behalf of English football, either on his own or with an organised FA/government group like the one which tried and failed to convince enough people that we should host the World Cup finals in 2006.

There was a period after the Munich air disaster in 1958 when he didn't seem to know which way he was going, as you would expect of someone who had survived but lost so many team-mates and close friends. He struggled to find consistency and played in various positions – outside-left, up front, in a deeper role. It was Sir Alf Ramsey who devised a way of playing Bobby in an England shirt: Alan Ball on the right with Nobby Stiles behind plus Martin

FACT FILE

FULL NAME: *Sir Robert Charlton CBE, OBE*

BORN: *11 October 1937, Ashington, Northumberland*

PLAYING CAREER
CLUBS: *Manchester United 1953-73; Preston North End 1974-75 (player-manager)*

APPEARANCES/GOALS:

	League	FA Cup	FL Cup	European
Man Utd	604(2)/199	78/19	24/7	45/22
Preston N.E.	38/8	4/1	3/1	

CAREER TOTAL: *796 (2) appearances/257 goals*

HONOURS: *First Division Champions 1956-57, 1964-65, 1966-67; FA Cup Winners 1963; FA Cup Finalists 1957, 1958; European Cup Winners 1967-68; European Footballer of the Year 1966; Footballer of the Year 1966; FA Youth Cup Winners 1954, 1955, 1956 (all with Manchester United)*

INTERNATIONAL: *England 106 appearances/49 goals, 1958-70*

HONOURS: *World Cup Winner 1966*

MANAGEMENT CAREER
CLUB: *Preston North End 1973-75*

OTHER: *Director of Manchester United 1984- ; PFA Merit Award 1974*

- Probably the most famous English player of all time, his name a global byword for Englishness.
- Blessed with exceptional pace and thunderous shooting power.
- Played more than 700 games for Manchester United, scoring close to 250 goals. Capped 106 times for his country and scored a record 49 international goals.
- With United, won the FA Youth Cup three times, the First Division title three times, the FA Cup and the European Cup.
- In 1966, was voted both the Footballer of the Year and the European Footballer of the Year.

Munich), championships and domestic cups. He played 106 times for England and scored a record 49 goals. In the process he won the hearts and minds of the people not just of his own land but everywhere the game is played. I suppose you could say he gives the impression of being stand-offish, a bit distant perhaps, maybe shy. But I always found him pleasant, approachable and good company, and he is one of the most respected and loved footballing men in the world.

I once worked on a commercial with him for Admiral, the sportswear company. It was great fun. My part was to walk

BELOW: **With brother Jack during England training at Stamford Bridge, April 1965.**

Peters to leave Bobby with a free role. It worked superbly well for a superb player.

You always felt with Bobby that you knew what he was going to do, but come the moment you couldn't stop him. He had incredible pace, blinding acceleration off the mark. There was also that feint of his, which he could do standing still: to the right with his left; left past the ball; then he was off. He hit shots with exceptional power. If they were on target the goalkeeper didn't stand a chance, unless he was lucky or it was just a little off target. I know of one Scottish keeper whose club trained against a then

> You always felt with Bobby that you knew what he was going to do, but come the moment you couldn't stop him.

English Football League representative side and who had always wanted to test himself against a Charlton shot. Here was his chance. He said afterwards, as he lay on the treatment table, that he remembered Charlton cocking his leg about twenty yards out, but nothing after that. He had stopped the shot with his face. Now that must have hurt!

Charlton won everything: the World Cup, the European Cup (which meant so much to him after

ABOVE: England's line-up for the April 1967 clash with Scotland. Bobby is seventh from the left.

He is instantly recognisable, probably the most recognisable Englishman after the Prime Minister, though I suspect Bobby would be more popular worldwide.

through a street market with Dennis Wise playing a taxi driver (naturally), leaning out of his cab window and shouting, 'All right, Tel!' If I can remember it exactly, David Seaman failed to catch a bag of apples thrown at him and I broke the local grocer's window with the ball. And who was the grocer? Sir Bobby Charlton, who stood there staring at me with a very unhappy look on his face, his hands on his hips. I recognised the pose.

Bobby didn't stay around long as a manager but he has put lots of work into his soccer schools that have encouraged talented youngsters to develop their skills and the less talented simply to enjoy the game. He is also a director of Manchester United, as he should be because his experience is unmatchable. He always seems to be on the move, jetting somewhere on some mission to represent his club or country and the game of football. He put a lot into trying to win that 2006 World Cup for England, and it was clear at the end that he felt frustrated and very disappointed when they lost the vote to a German campaign fronted by Franz Beckenbauer. Nevertheless, like the Kaiser in Germany, Sir Robert Charlton CBE OBE remains a national treasure.

Gordon Banks

England's Greatest Goalkeeper

GORDON BANKS WAS ONE OF THE FINEST GOALKEEPERS IN THE HISTORY OF THE GAME. SOME PEOPLE MAY SAY PETER SHILTON WAS THE BETTER KEEPER BECAUSE HE WON 125 CAPS COMPARED TO GORDON'S 73, AND IT IS TRUE BOTH PLAYERS WERE BRILLIANT.

But to me Gordon Banks had the edge for the simple reason that England won a World Cup with him between the sticks. Perhaps that's unfair, but it's how I see it. For several years after England had won the World Cup in 1966, Gordon was regarded as the best keeper in the world.

Gordon was a native of Sheffield but both clubs missed out on him and he signed for Chesterfield, a club that at that time had a strong reputation for its 'goalkeeping academy'. Gordon was strong, primarily because he had worked as a coal-bagger at the local pit. He quickly made a name for himself in the Chesterfield junior sides, helping them to reach the

final of the FA Youth Cup in 1955/56, which they lost 3-4 on aggregate to Manchester United's famous youth side containing Bobby Charlton and Wilf McGuiness, both future England players.

Chesterfield were unable to resist an offer of £7,000 for Gordon, and in 1959 he moved to Leicester City. Leicester's new manager, Matt Gillies, put Banks straight into the first team. Frank McLintock was also introduced at this time. Both would be in the Leicester team that reached the FA Cup final in 1961. Tottenham won that final, but not before Gordon had proved himself an outstanding talent, denying Spurs until just 20 minutes before the end.

> It's nice to say I have scored past one of the greatest goalkeepers ever.

Gordon made his international debut against Scotland at Wembley in 1963. His greatest day was to arrive three years later when England beat West Germany 4-2 after extra time at Wembley to take the World Cup for the first and so far only time. Banks' contribution to that success cannot be exaggerated because he gave the defence a supreme confidence by his very presence. Absolutely sure in everything he did, he possessed astonishing reflexes that enabled him to make seemingly impossible saves.

For my money, Gordon was one of the three greatest England players, along with Bobby Moore and Bobby Charlton. I played against

LEFT: **Another acrobatic save in the World Cup final, July 1966.**

ABOVE: **Finalising his World Cup preparation, June 1966.**

FACT FILE

FULL NAME: *Gordon Banks*

BORN: *30 December 1937, Sheffield*

PLAYING CAREER
CLUBS: *Chesterfield 1955–59; Leicester City 1959–67; Stoke City 1967–73; Fort Lauderdale Strikers (USA) 1973–75*

APPEARANCES:

	League	FA Cup	FL Cup	European
Chesterfield	23			
Leicester City	293	34	25	4
Stoke City	194	27	19	6
Fort Lauderdale	*not available*			

CAREER TOTAL: *625 appearances*

HONOURS: *FA Cup Finalist 1961, 1963 (with Leicester City); League Cup Winners 1964 (with Leicester City), 1972 (with Stoke City); Footballer of the Year 1972*

INTERNATIONAL: *England 73 appearances, 1963–72*

HONOURS: *World Cup Winner 1966*

Absolutely sure in everything he did, he possessed astonishing reflexes that enabled him to make seemingly impossible saves.

Many feel that Gordon Banks' finest hour was in Mexico in 1970 when England defended their World Cup crown. In hostile conditions, searing heat combined with the high altitude to cause the players to lose over half a stone in weight in the course of 90 minutes. It was in the group stage match against Brazil that Banks made his supreme save from Pele's certain goal. Even Pele congratulated Banks. The Brazilian could not believe it – his header was pin-pointed accurately down towards the ground, it bounced upwards and Banks had to throw himself back and get the ball up and over the bar. Gordon's strength and timing were immaculate.

However, Banks was absent from the crucial quarter-final against old foe West Germany. He was suffering from food poisoning and there were

Gordon for Chelsea in the League Cup final of 1965, and I scored a penalty against him. I knew the odds were in my favour but it was still Gordon Banks in goal so I was certainly feeling pressured. It's nice to say I have scored past one of the greatest goalkeepers ever. Gordon was not only a great goalkeeper, he was also a nice guy.

I always got on with him. Like Bobby Moore, he got to the top of his profession; Gordon was always ice cool, never got rattled, was always in control.

98   Terry Venables' Football Heroes

> Like Bobby Moore, Gordon got to the top of his profession; he was always ice cool, never got rattled, was always in control.

rumours that his food or drink had been spiked before the game. Peter Bonetti (who I think was a fantastic keeper) was Gordon's stand-in, but Peter didn't have a great game, and West Germany eventually won 3-2, despite seeming certain losers when England were 2-0 up. Gordon's absence was keenly felt, although some blamed Alf Ramsey's substitution of Bobby Charlton, designed to save Bobby for the semi-final. Either way, England were out of the World Cup.

The season after winning the Footballer of the Year award in 1972, Gordon, now aged 35, was involved in a terrible car crash in a head-on collision with a van. It resulted in him losing the sight in his right eye. His first class career was over.

Gordon was a football purist and he didn't enjoy his two seasons with Fort Lauderdale over in the USA. In spite of the financial rewards, he said he felt like a fairground attraction – 'Roll up, roll up. See the best one-eyed goalie in the world.'

Gordon was without question a great player and a great bloke, and someone I have wonderful and fond memories of. He is a gentleman in the Bobby Moore mould, like most of the players in the 1966 England squad. The sixties was a time when playing for your country was a source of great pride and joy. Perhaps it still is today, but commercial interests have undoubtedly also made their mark.

BELOW: **Gordon throws himself into England training, March 1969. His dedication was absolutely outstanding.**

THE VENABLES VERDICT

- *For my money, the greatest England goalkeeper of all time.*
- *Always gave the defence a supreme confidence by his very presence.*
- *A pivotal figure in England's 1966 World Cup glory.*
- *Made arguably the greatest save ever, from Pele's downward header in the 1970 Mexico World Cup.*
- *A great player and a great bloke.*

Denis Law

The Mischievous Schoolboy

DENIS LAW WAS AS MUCH ABOUT PERSONALITY AS PLAYING ABILITY. HE WAS A GREAT CHARACTER. HE STRODE ON TO THE PITCH AS THOUGH HE OWNED IT. HE WAS COCKY AND CONFIDENT, WITH HIS HEAD ALWAYS HELD HIGH. HE WAS A HELL OF A PLAYER TO HAVE ON YOUR SIDE.

I think it was his air of schoolboy mischievousness that endeared him to the crowds. He was like someone out of a *Just William* book – you always expected him to do something completely irreverent and very funny.

He was immensely brave, abrasive, fearlessly combative, with two wonderful feet and an awesome ability in the air which made him the scourge of defences throughout Europe. He came in for terrible

> ### He was like someone out of a *Just William* book – you always expected him to do something completely irreverent.

physical abuse from defenders, his fiery temperament often landing him in trouble as he eventually snapped, retaliating violently. Of course, the defenders knew all about his temper, so they would just wind him up, snapping at his heels like a terrier worrying a cat.

His volatile character saw him twice suspended for four weeks. On one of these occasions, during the 1963/64 season, he returned with a bang. With a wonderful sense of theatre he scored four goals in his first game back from suspension, one for each week he had been away. He walked off the Old Trafford pitch to a standing ovation, grinning broadly in that cheeky way of his, holding up four fingers.

RIGHT: Denis finds himself smothered by Gordon Banks in an England/Scotland match in April 1967.

There is no doubt that he played to the crowd. In that season, despite his 'midwinter holiday' as he described it, he scored 46 goals (30 in the League, ten in the FA Cup and six in the European Cup-Winners' Cup), a record for the club. His tally included a remarkable seven hat-tricks.

But as a boy you would never have believed that he would grow up to be a top sportsman. He was small and extremely thin with a pronounced squint in his right eye. To combat the squint he always played with his right eye closed. One day his life changed and he was on his way to the big time. Andy Beattie was manager of Huddersfield Town in the early to mid-1950s and his brother Archie was used as a scout in Scotland. Archie spotted the young Law playing for Aberdeen Boys and recommended him to his brother, arranging for Denis to travel down for a trial.

Bill Shankly was Beattie's assistant at this time and Law knocked on his door when he arrived at the ground. Shankly couldn't believe his eyes as this tiny, skinny boy with spiky hair, National Health glasses with a patch and a decided squint in one eye stepped in to the room and announced, 'I'm Denis Law'. Shankly thought Archie had been on the booze, so he sent the lad round to the training pitch where the first team were having their weekly practice match against the reserves, meaning to ring Archie to ask what the hell he was doing.

Half an hour later the first team captain burst into Bill Shankly's office blabbing something about the scrawny young Scottish lad. Shankly began to apologise, but the captain was not listening – he was too busy telling his boss that none of the first team defence could get the ball off Denis and the reserves were winning by several goals.

It was the start of a great mutual respect between Shankly and Law. Shankly would indulge Denis like he would indulge no other player. Bill Shankly was

> ## Bill Shankly was not someone you messed with but he cared about Denis.

not someone you messed with but he cared about Denis. Matt Busby of Manchester United tried to buy Law when he was 16 for what was then the massive sum of £10,000, but Shankly wouldn't sell his gem.

There is a wonderful story that sums up the relationship between Shankly and Law. Denis had been away and was due back on a certain date. The date came and went – no Denis. When he failed to appear Bill Shankly asked his assistant Bob Paisley where Denis was. But Paisley didn't know either. Shankly was furious because Huddersfield had a big game coming up and he felt that Denis was being disrespectful towards the club. If all the other players could take it seriously then why couldn't he?

Shankly decided he would give Denis a real tongue-lashing, but he had to get it just right, so he asked Paisley to go outside and play the part of Denis Law. Paisley went outside, knocked on the door and when Shankly said come in, he entered the room. Shankly told him, 'Now Denis, this isn't good enough. You have to respect the club. You can't just disappear and not return when you

BELOW: **A typically surging run in the colours of Manchester City.**

FACT FILE

FULL NAME: *Denis Law*

BORN: *24 February 1940, Aberdeen*

PLAYING CAREER
CLUBS: *Huddersfield Town 1955–60; Manchester City 1960–61, 1973–74; Torino (Italy) 1961–62; Manchester United 1962–73*

APPEARANCES/GOALS:

	League	FA Cup	FL Cup	European
Huddersfield Town	81/16	10/2		
Manchester City	66(2)/30	5/4	6/3	
Torino	27/10			
Manchester United	305(4)/171	44(2)/34	11/3	33/28

CAREER TOTAL: *558(8) appearances/301 goals*

HONOURS: *First Division Champions 1964–65, 1966–67 (with Manchester United); FA Cup Winners 1963 (with Manchester United); European Footballer of the Year 1964; League Cup Finalists 1973–74 (with Manchester City)*

INTERNATIONAL: *Scotland 55 appearances/30 goals, 1958–74 (Scottish record, shared with Kenny Dalglish); Rest of World v. England 1963*

Despite the close attention of Derby County's Roy McFarland and Colin Todd, Denis fires a shot goalbound.

say you will.' But Shankly was not happy so they tried it again, with a different, firmer approach. 'Now Denis, I'll have to let you go if this continues, you can't let the club down.' But still it didn't seem right so they tried again. Shankly was determined that this time Denis Law would not get away with it. 'This is not good enough, Denis. I'll have to take action. It's not fair on the other players.' Still no good. So Shankly sent Paisley out of the room one more time. There was a knock on the door and instead of Paisley, in walked Denis. Shankly leapt to his feet, rushed round to the other side of the desk and clasped Denis to his chest. 'Denis, where have you been?'

But eventually Shankly did let him go when Manchester City paid a British record £55,000 for the 19-year-old Denis in March 1960. Some thought it was a surprising decision by Law because City were perpetual First Division strugglers, but his fantastic energy and stamina carried him to all parts of the pitch as he tried to plug the many gaps in City's side.

THE VENABLES VERDICT

- A great character. Cocky and confident with a schoolboy mischievousness.

- A volatile individual whose fiery temper sometimes got him into trouble on the pitch.

- At Huddersfield Town, Bill Shankly indulged Denis like no other player.

- A supreme goal poacher who, unusually, played for both Manchester teams.

In 1962 Denis went to Italy to play for Torino but he never settled there. He returned the following year to Manchester United and he shone. Matt Busby used him as a striker where his instincts for being in the right place at the right time brought him masses of goals. He was the supreme poacher.

Denis was a wonderfully plucky little player. As far as I am concerned, he was a truly great character who brought colour and life to the clubs he played for, the people he met and those who watched him play.

Pele

A God-given Talent

T HE FIRST TIME I SAW PELE PLAY WAS IN THE 1958 WORLD CUP FINALS. HE WAS STILL ONLY 17, BUT HE WAS ELECTRIFYING. HE MADE US ALL SIT UP AND REALISE THAT THIS WAS SOMEONE SPECIAL. IN FACT, I'D NEVER SEEN A FOOTBALLER LIKE IT.

He scored his first World Cup goal against Wales in the quarter-final and followed this with a sensational hat-trick against France in the semi-final. In the final itself Brazil beat the host nation Sweden 5-2 and Pele scored twice to achieve instant world fame.

His philosophy can be summed up in his own comment about the game: 'Football is like a religion to me. I worship the ball and treat it like a god. Too many players think of a football as something to kick. They should be taught to caress it and treat it like a precious gem!'

There still exists some amazing footage from that

Pele's appearance in a match in Africa caused a two-day truce to be called in the Biafra-Nigeria war

tournament of Pele casting his magic spell before volleying the ball into the net with an ease you could not believe. It was as if someone from Mars had landed. I'd never seen such natural talent, and it was combined with such a pure love of the game.

When Pele returned to Brazil after the 1958 World Cup, his club Santos quickly realised they had a hot property, so they decided to take advantage of this fact. Santos became football's version of the Harlem Globetrotters, touring the world, playing lucrative friendly matches two or three times a week, building up sufficient funds to buy the best players to set around their 'crown jewel'. Santos won the World Club Championship in 1962 and 1963.

During my playing career I once travelled in a car from London to Sheffield to watch him play for Santos against Sheffield Wednesday in an exhibition match at Hillsborough. The stadium was absolutely packed, and Pele was astounding. His technical ability was unique. When he took a penalty, it was the most amazing thing I had seen. He ran towards the ball and then stopped and balanced on one leg; he waited for the goalkeeper to move and then struck the ball the other side. He came 'inside' the ball and hit it, which meant he could prod the ball as opposed to just hitting it straight. But it was the way he charged at the ball and then just froze. I have never witnessed anything like it before or since. He just stopped as if in a photograph.

RIGHT: **A wonderful moment from the 1970 Mexico World Cup. Pele and Bobby Moore display their huge mutual respect.**

LEFT: **A spectacular overhead kick against Belgium in Rio from July 1964.**

He was a true genius and I think his talent is as inspirational as any other artist's.

The goalkeeper flew across the goal-mouth and Pele coolly tucked the ball into the opposite corner. The stadium just erupted. It was one of those moments that you know will stay with you forever.

Pele once said, 'A penalty is a cowardly way to score.' Maybe. But with Pele taking it, it was spectacular and very entertaining.

Of course, the way that Pele took that penalty would not be permitted now – another example of the over-complicated rules that I believe infest football these days. The relevant rule states that if the goalkeeper moves forward before the ball is struck, the penalty can be taken again; but the player cannot stop in his stride. I think it is best to allow the play-

er to stop and the goalkeeper to move. After all, if the keeper knows the penalty taker can stop and make him look fool-ish, then he's not going to move

LEFT: **The characteristic drop of the shoulder and a perfect nutmeg. Another defender completely bamboozled.**

is he? I doubt if most players will stop, so it solves the problem. Why does the game have to be complicated by rules like this? My philosophy is always, 'Keep it simple'.

I played against Pele once when I was young and with Chelsea. He was just the most amazing player. We finally met up when we were both involved with the kit manufacturer Umbro's 'Star Chamber' for a discussion on where the game was going and what it would be like in ten years' time. He was the nicest man you could meet, very unassuming.

Luis Van Gaal, who had just won the European Cup as manager of Ajax, was there too, I recall. He was full of himself. We were being taken round Charleston in the USA in a horse-drawn carriage. My wife Toots and I were sitting in the back next to Pele and his partner, with Van Gaal and his wife up front next to the driver of the carriage. Suddenly, we passed by two Ajax supporters wearing their club shirt – slap-bang in the middle of America, thou-sands of miles from home. Luis Van Gaal said, 'Stop. Stop the horses. Stop the horses.' So the driver brought us to a standstill and the Dutchman jumped down from the carriage and rushed up to the sup-porters shouting 'Yeah, we did it.' The fans hugged him. Van Gaal returned to the carriage and said to us, 'What do you think?' I told him, 'I'm impressed. That's the first case of the manager recognising the fan, rather than the fan recognising the manager.' Pele started to laugh; he thought it was really funny. Van Gaal behaved like that throughout the trip – I'd like to think it's eccentricity rather than arrogance. Pele, the real superstar, was very understated.

Van Gaal was a great manager but not a star play-er. Once he had made his name as a coach he met Pele and said, 'Remember me?' Pele told him he did not. Van Gaal persisted and explained, 'I played against you many years ago and when you were on the pitch and close to me, I put the ball through your legs and then I picked it up round the other side, remember?' Pele just laughed and said, 'I don't believe that for one minute. I don't remember you and you certainly didn't put the ball between my legs.' Van Gaal sighed, 'Ah, OK. But it's true.'

It was very funny and Van Gaal kept us all entertained without even realising that he was being funny. He was the complete opposite of Pele. The Brazilian never boasted about his abilities. He was a true genius and I think his talent is as inspirational as any other artist's. He once said, 'I was born for soccer, just as Beethoven was born for music.' I couldn't agree more. His skill has given millions of football fans pleasure just as Beethoven has given millions of music lovers pleasure. They are both God-given talents.

Pele's finest moment was probably at the 1970 World Cup. The group-stage match against England was judged to be one of the greatest games ever. The now famous personal duel between Pele and Bobby Moore was certainly one of the highlights – the greatest striker against the greatest defender. Both men were gentlemen so it was a duel of skill not rough tactics. When you witness it for the first time, you realise just how rare that kind of skill is. It was a pity that Brazil did not meet England in the final, because I reckon that might have made for the greatest game of all time. Unfortunately, it was not to be – England were knocked out in the quarter-final stage. Brazil won the final by overcoming Italy 4-1, Pele scoring the crucial first goal. At the end of this tournament it was widely acknowledged that Brazil had elevated football to an art form. Undoubtedly, they had.

Pele was always more than just a footballer. When he retired, the world governing body FIFA

FACT FILE

FULL NAME: *Edson Arantes do Nascimento*

BORN: *21 October 1940, Três Coraçoes, Minas Gerais, Brazil*

PLAYING CAREER

CLUBS: *Noroeste (Brazil) 1954–56; Santos (Brazil) 1956–74; New York Cosmos (USA) 1974–77*

APPEARANCES/GOALS: *1,363 matches/1,283 goals*

INTERNATIONAL: *Brazil 91 appearances/78 goals, 1957–71 (also played in 20 'A' internationals, 19 goals)*

HONOURS: *World Cup Winner 1958, 1970 (with Brazil); World Club Champions 1962, 1963 (with Santos); South American Clubs Cup Winners 1962, 1963 (with Santos); Sao Paulo State Champions 1956, 1958, 1960, 1961, 1962, 1964, 1965, 1967, 1968, 1969, 1973 (with Santos); Brazilian Cup Winners 1962, 1963, 1964, 1965 (with Santos); Sao Paulo Tournament Winners 1959, 1963, 1964; Roberto Gomez Pedrosa Tournament Winners 1968; South American Footballer of the Year 1973; appointed Brazil's Minister for Sport 1994*

acknowledged his magnetism by appointing him as their roving ambassador, his presence adding dignity and credibility to every occasion. His appearance in a match in Africa caused a two-day truce to be called in the Biafra-Nigeria war – everyone then had the opportunity to watch the great Pele play.

His is the legendary 'rags to riches' story. He was born impoverished, the son of a poorly-paid Brazilian professional footballer nicknamed 'Dondino'. But Pele blossomed under his father's coaching, the latter developing his son's incredible natural talent. It is strange, but often the greatest sportsmen are sons of the 'not quite made it' fathers. These dads have some talent that seems to be passed down ten-fold to their sons.

OPPOSITE: **Proudly holding aloft the 1970 World Cup trophy.**

RIGHT: **The great man is now a roving ambassador for FIFA, the sport's world governing body.**

The poor boy from the back streets received the ultimate accolade when he was invited by the Brazilian government to become the country's Minister for Sport. In that role he succeeded in getting passed what became known as 'Pele's Law'. The ruling reformed the organisation of Brazilian domestic football that had exploited its indigenous players mercilessly over the years.

Pele will leave behind him the legacy of a player who transcended football to become not only a superb sportsman but also a wonderful person. He was respected by friend and foe alike.

He was the ultimate footballer.

It was as if someone from Mars had landed. I'd never seen such natural talent, and it was combined with such a pure love of the game.

THE VENABLES VERDICT

- *A really special player, blessed with unique skills. The ultimate footballer.*

- *Won the World Cup twice with Brazil, in 1958 and 1970.*

- *Burst on to the international scene during the 1958 World Cup tournament, scoring a hat-trick in the semi-final and two more in the final.*

- *Voted 'The Player of the Century' in a recent FIFA poll.*

- *Has acted as his country's Minister for Sport, and as FIFA's roving ambassador.*

- *Never boasted about his abilities. Hugely modest.*

- *Once said, 'A penalty is a cowardly way to score.'*

Bobby Moore

An Absolute Gentleman

PELE HAS DESCRIBED BOBBY MOORE AS THE FINEST DEFENDER IN THE WORLD: ACCOLADES DO NOT COME ANY HIGHER THAN THAT. BOBBY WAS ARGUABLY ENGLAND'S GREATEST DEFENDER AND THE GREATEST CAPTAIN; CERTAINLY THE ONLY CAPTAIN IN THIS COUNTRY'S HISTORY TO LIFT THE WORLD CUP ON THAT FAMOUS SUMMER'S AFTERNOON IN 1966.

I first met Bobby when I was about 15. He was a couple of years older than me. We would go training in the evenings and then go to a little East London café called Casse Ttari. It was owned by an Italian and we had bacon sandwiches and a couple of mugs of tea. The bus stop was right outside, and my wife Toots lived in the road opposite. Her mum still lives there today.

One day I bumped into Bobby in the café. In those days football players didn't earn very much money – nothing like the amount they earn today – so we could only just about scrape together enough

> ### His coolness under intense pressure was remarkable, his distribution of the ball rarely inaccurate.

to pay for the bacon sandwiches and tea. Bobby paid for my meal that day – that epitomises the kind of person he was. He was always generous and always thinking about other people.

He had this certain detached air about him which made people think he was stand-offish. But he was not like that at all, he was always ready to chat. For most of us at that time our life revolved around that café. We would train, eat and then go home. We thought, ate and slept football. There was no other way to be. If you were born in the East End of London the temptation was to do something different with your life. Very early on I realised this and focussed hard on my football.

The sixties was a time when class barriers were coming down and people like Terry O'Neill and David Bailey were just as likely to be invited to Buckingham Palace as they were to the Old Kent Road. It was fun, exciting and Bobby was right at the centre of it. When England won the World Cup in 1966, life changed; football was suddenly trendy and everyone wanted to be part of it. Of course, Bobby was at the head of the guest list, and he

BELOW: **Dejection is written all over the faces of Bobby and Alf Ramsey after the defeat by West Germany in the 1970 World Cup finals.**

represented England and the football world immaculately. He was always an absolute gentleman, as happy talking to royalty as to any man in the street. He never lost touch with his roots.

One thing that always struck me about Bobby was his elegance, his dress sense. He always looked fabulously well turned out. I shared a room with him once and everything was kept so tidy. We were coaching together in South Africa with Bill McGarry, the manager of Wolves, and Geoff Hurst. The Bobby factor rubbed off on me and by the end of the coaching contract I was folding everything and putting it away neatly in the drawers and hanging things in the wardrobe. It didn't last long, though, and I was soon back to normal when I got home. I think it was too much of a shock to my family and friends who knew just how naturally untidy I was. Anyway I couldn't keep it up. It's just not me.

Bobby's self-discipline was as evident on the pitch as off it. He overcame his weaknesses and with sheer determination turned himself into one of the finest defenders in the history of the game. Playing in the old defensive left-half position, he possessed an unsurpassed vision that enabled him to be ahead of any situation that might arise. He never seemed to be in a hurry and timed his tackling to perfection, never resorting to 'professional fouls'. His coolness under the most intense pressure was remarkable, his distribution of the ball unfussy and rarely inaccurate. His *pièce de résistance* was seeing the forward pass so early – a dream for an attacker.

Many modern players should take a leaf out of Bobby's book. Dedication and discipline get you a long way, so long as you harness it with your natural talent, which Bobby had in abundance. Pure unharnessed genius, however, soon burns itself out.

His duels with Pele and the other Brazilian strikers in the 1970 World Cup are now legendary. Bobby's cool eye enabled him to tackle even the world's greatest player as clean as a whistle, with not a hint of a foul. I believe videos of those games

BELOW: **Bobby is flanked by West Ham team-mates Geoff Hurst and Martin Peters.**

should be compulsory viewing for today's generation of defenders.

I think Bobby was lucky that at West Ham he came under the influence of Malcolm Allison, who coached the young players. Football was changing but many clubs refused to acknowledge the fact. They coached young players in an old-fashioned way, rather than allowing them to develop in the more forward-thinking, free-flowing approach that was becoming popular. Malcolm Allison was a football visionary and Bobby quickly blossomed under his tutelage.

Senior players, members of West Ham's famous 'academy of football thinkers' like Noel Cantwell, were also great influences on the young Moore. From Noel, Bobby learned how to substitute pace for intelligence, and how to read the

ABOVE: **Receiving the Jules Rimet Trophy from the Queen, 30 July 1966.**

> **I don't think many realised how ill he was because he kept up appearances until the very end.**

game and maximise his skills and particular approach to the game.

He was soon recognised at England youth level, then picked for the England Under-23 team. In 1962 he was the surprise choice for England's tour of South America, making his international debut against Peru in May.

For Bobby, football was everything. He married quite young and went to Mallorca on honeymoon. After a few days he discovered that Malcolm Allison and Noel Cantwell were also on holiday there. One night he disappeared to their villa, spending the whole night discussing football theory, much to his young wife's annoyance. But that was Bobby – once he got into a discussion about his beloved game, he would mull over the various theories and discuss various methods and new ways of doing things literally all night. He was an insomniac, so sleep was not important to him.

Bobby became England's most capped player with 108 appearances for his country, 90 as captain. In 1967 he was awarded the OBE. He was a wonderful asset to the game in every way. I'll never understand why he wasn't knighted. In my opinion, the FA should have asked Bobby to act as its ambassador. Apparently, they didn't ask Bobby because they feared it would set a precedent. Strange, I thought, when I heard this. I don't remember too many other World Cup-winning captains in England's history.

In his playing days I didn't see that much of Bobby but later we started spending time together, going out to dinner pretty regularly. I always enjoyed

Bobby was always an absolute gentleman, as happy talking to royalty as to any man on the street. He never lost touch with his roots.

an evening with Bobby. He had a good sense of humour and a liking for a beer or two. I can recall some raucous evenings spent with our respective wives. Great times.

I think people were surprised when he left his beloved West Ham in 1974. He joined Fulham and guided his new club to the FA Cup final in 1975, against his old club. In every fairy story there is a happy ending, but this one saw a 2-0 victory for East over West London.

Regrettably, Bobby's own life did not have a happy ending. Colon cancer took him at the tragically early age of 51. His death left us all inconsolable and the football world in a state of grief. He was such a dignified man with an iron will that I

don't think many realised how ill he was because he kept up appearances until the very end. In fact, he was supposed to have lunch with us one weekend at Bobby and Jan Keetch's house. It was Toots and me, Maria and Jeff Powell (of the *Daily Mail*) and of course Bobby and Stephanie. Stephanie called to say that Bobby didn't want to let us down but he was not well. A couple of days later he died. That was typical of Bobby. He died as he lived his life – with understated elegance.

Bobby Moore and Bobby Keetch were two of my best friends. Bobby and Stephanie and Toots and I got married in December 1991 within a week of each other. We were a close-knit support unit. Yet my two great mates both died within a few short years of each other. They left a big gap in my life. True friends are hard to come by.

When Bobby died his wife Stephanie became very involved with the Bobby Moore Fund for Imperial Cancer Research and her efforts have raised over £1 million. Bobby would have been very proud of that and would have undoubtedly admired her tenacity and fortitude in the face of such a great loss. I think when Bobby died we all reflected on our lives and tried in some way to take on some of his generosity and selflessness. He was an example to us, his

THE VENABLES VERDICT

- *Always a gentleman. Never lost touch with his roots.*
- *Generous and selfless – an example to us all.*
- *Possessed wonderful vision and a great coolness under pressure.*
- *Timed his tackling to perfection.*
- *Skippered England to World Cup glory in 1966.*

friends and to everyone he met.

My most abiding memory of Bobby is of him wiping the mud off his hands at Wembley before he shook hands with the Queen, so he would not soil her white gloves. He then received the World Cup from her. That was typical of Bobby. Even in a moment of great personal triumph and happiness, he still had a keen sense of 'place' and good manners.

ABOVE: **Yet another perfectly-executed tackle, this time for Fulham against Sheffield United's Keith Edwards.**

Franz Beckenbauer

The Kaiser

FRANZ BECKENBAUER WASN'T BORN WITH A SILVER SPOON IN HIS MOUTH, BUT IT SEEMED LIKE IT TO THE REST OF A FOOTBALL WORLD THAT WATCHED IN AWE AS THE GREAT MAN'S CAREER UNFURLED – PERFECTLY, DARE I SAY EFFORTLESSLY. I SPEAK WITH RESPECT, NOT ENVY, BUT EVERYTHING TOUCHED BY HIM HAS BEEN A GLOBAL SUCCESS.

Elegant, sophisticated, highly intelligent, a wonderful, innovative footballer, the 'Kaiser' is a man of many talents. Nothing should be so straightforward, but his life has been relatively scandal-free, and even when one broke so surprisingly over his head recently he had the guts to face it, not try to hide or blame it all on others.

When I think of Franz I have this picture in my mind of him with the late Bobby Moore and Pele at their prime. They were the stars of their generation, and having met as rivals in deeply emotional games, major World Cup ties, they became friends who never lost touch. It was Franz who spoke at Bobby's memorial service at Westminster Abbey and in doing so he paid his own personal tribute to a man for whom he had a great regard.

The mention of Beckenbauer's name also brings to mind one of Sir Alf Ramsey's big mistakes during the 1970 World Cup finals in Mexico. Bobby Charlton was making life very uncomfortable for the Kaiser – he was one of the few who was able to unsettle him – and England looked good for a win when Sir Alf decided to sub Bobby prematurely, assuming the game was over. He was very wrong. The initiative was handed back to the West Germans, Beckenbauer recovered his game and England went out of the competition.

Those who never watched Beckenbauer in action may have difficulty in believing how superb a player he was. Trust me, he was something else again. He did everything from a very young age. He played in the West Germany side beaten by Bobby Moore's England team in

LEFT: **Lifting the 1974 World Cup alongside goalkeeper Sepp Maier.**

the 1966 World Cup, and did so with a dashing style. He epitomised what was to be known as the 'sweeper' role. He was one of the first, and few would begrudge calling him the greatest. As a player, Franz had the ability to control the tempo of a game by using his passing skills to switch defence into attack

> We have had reason to curse his inspired football, but you must also respect and admire one of the greatest players the world has seen.

FACT FILE

FULL NAME: *Franz Beckenbauer*

BORN: *11 September 1945, Munich*

PLAYING CAREER

CLUBS: *Bayern Munich 1958-77; New York Cosmos 1977-80, 1983; SV Hamburg 1980-82*

APPEARANCES/GOALS:

	League	Cup	European
Bayern Munich	*427/61*	*61/5*	*72/6*
SV Hamburg	*28/0*		
New York Cosmos	*132/22*		

CAREER TOTAL: *720 appearances/94 goals*

HONOURS: *Bundesliga Champions 1968-69, 1972-73, 1973-74, 1974-75; German Cup Winners 1966, 1967, 1969, 1971; European Cup Winners 1973-74, 1974-75, 1975-76; European Cup-Winners' Cup Winners 1966-67; European Footballer of the Year 1972, 1976 (all with Bayern Munich); NAFL Super Bowl Winners 1978, 1980 (with New York Cosmos)*

INTERNATIONAL: *West Germany 104 appearances/15 goals, 1965-81*

HONOURS: *World Cup Winner 1974; World Cup Finalist 1966; European Championship Winner 1972*

MANAGEMENT CAREER

CLUBS: *West Germany 1984-90; Olympique Marseille 1990; Bayern Munich 1993-94*

HONOURS: *World Cup Winners 1990 (with Germany); World Cup Finalists 1986 (with West Germany); Bundesliga Champions 1993-94 (with Bayern Munich)*

OTHERS: *Senior Executive, Bayern Munich 1994-96; President, Bayern Munich 1996-*

in an instant. He had pace too, remarkable pace, and he used it to bring the ball out of defence so quickly that it often caught the opposition cold and unprepared. But not everybody had the knowledge to appreciate Franz's style of play, especially in America where they tend to cover up ignorance with a big mouth. One New York Cosmos executive just couldn't understand what Beckenbauer was trying to achieve by playing so deep. Hadn't they paid a lot of money for this German? This message was relayed to the coach: 'Tell the Kraut to get his ass up front! We don't pay a million for a guy to hang around in defence!' Can you believe it?

Franz literally guaranteed success – success with the German national side (one win from two World Cup finals as a player), with Bayern Munich (three European Cup final victories, several German championship and cup wins, the European Cup-Winners' Cup) and as an individual player (two European Footballer of the Year awards). There was also a North American Soccer League Super Bowl win with the star-spangled Cosmos, though his spell at Hamburg was the least productive in terms of titles. He walked into managing the national side and naturally won the World Cup for them in 1990, becoming the first man to win the world title as player and manager. He flirted with Marseilles, then rejoined his former club Bayern where he is now, as you would expect, President of the 2001 Champions League winners.

BELOW: **Franz was a key figure in the development of the North American Soccer League.**

We were acquaintances and our paths have crossed frequently over the years, like they did in Mexico during a pre-World Cup tournament in 1984/85 when I was coach of Barcelona. I was sitting talking to friends in Mexico City's Camino Real Hotel when I was told there was a telephone call for me. I

> He epitomised what was to be known as the 'sweeper' role. He was one of the first, and few would begrudge calling him the greatest.

asked who it was; 'Franz Beckenbauer' came the reply. My friends laughed and my first thought was that it was a wind-up. But it was definitely Franz, and he wanted my help with my Barcelona player Bernd Schuster who had refused to play for his country. Franz phoned me a number of times over the next few days, much to the amusement of my friends. To this day, if I take a call with them around they'll chorus 'Franz for you again!' A big joke, but the episode showed that it wasn't beneath him to ask for help.

I once watched him play in Switzerland with his arm in a sling. How the heck can he do that?, I asked myself. Your arm helps you balance – it is essential. But I should have known better than to question, even to myself, anything Franz Beckenbauer tried. If my memory is correct, he not only played that day as gracefully as always but scored a couple of goals too. Perhaps having one of his legs in a sling would make a difference.

The Germans gave Franz the nickname the Kaiser. It is their acknowledgement of a man they regard as their emperor, the most influential figure on the German football scene since the mid-sixties, very possibly their most influential football figure ever. We have had reason to curse his inspired football, but you must also respect and admire one of the greatest players the world has seen.

ABOVE LEFT: **Gracefully avoiding a stiff Polish challenge during the 1974 World Cup finals.**

THE VENABLES VERDICT

- *An elegant, dashing, highly intelligent and innovative footballer.*

- *One of the first true 'sweepers', expert at switching defence into attack in an instant.*

- *Glittering club career with Bayern Munich – four Bundesliga titles, four German Cups, three European Cups and a European Cup-Winners' Cup.*

- *Fantastic international record – 104 caps, 15 goals, one World Cup and one European Championship.*

- *As a manager, took his country to two World Cup finals (winning one) and his beloved Bayern to a Bundesliga title.*

George Best

Pure Gifts

T HEY SAY THAT GEORGE BEST WAS A WAYWARD IRISH GENIUS, AND HE HAS BEEN WIDELY ACCLAIMED AS THE BEST PLAYER EVER PRODUCED WITHIN THE BRITISH ISLES. I THINK THAT'S TRUE.

He was given a gift of incredible talent which was allowed to flourish under the guidance of Sir Matt Busby, rather than be stifled by rigid coaching. It was a pity he didn't last as long as he should have at Manchester United. I think he left the club when he was only 27.

They say he was better than Gascoigne, but then Gascoigne plays on into his thirties, and although his career has been affected by rough challenges and reckless off-pitch behaviour, I don't think Gazza would ever want to walk away from the game. It's his life. Maybe the worst thing for George was that the explosive combination of unbelievable talent and good looks gave him a dilemma in life: was he a footballer or a superstar? George certainly enjoyed the other side of life, the nightclubs and the girls, in a manner that wasn't good for his football.

But back to the football. George was a player

> **There is no doubt that he made football a richer sport with his wonderful, unadulterated talent.**

whom the crowds flocked to see. He was gifted beyond belief, his skill on the ball impossible to describe as helpless defenders were left floundering in his wake. He could tackle, he was a left- and right-footed player, he was loved by his team-mates and was a very good team player. Players like Pele, Maradona and Gascoigne, along with Best, were all individuals, and normally in life people don't like individuals and are jealous of them, but the really great players like those I've mentioned, the great

givers, don't want to be treated as anything special. They are revered by the players. Players don't get jealous of the likes of Bobby Moore, Johnny Haynes, Alfredo di Stefano and Johan Cruyff because not only are they brilliant individuals but brilliant team players as well.

George's life began in a working-class housing estate in Belfast. He was a small, shy boy who had inherited the genes of his mother, who had been an Irish international hockey player. From a very young age he constantly had a ball at his feet, and he played for his school and local youth club. Manchester United had a number of scouts in Ireland in the early sixties, and one of them recognised the small lad's extraordinary talent. After discussions with his parents, who knew of United's reputation for

BELOW: **Getting the better of Chelsea's Ron 'Chopper' Harris.**

looking after young boys, it was agreed that the fifteen-year-old George could go to Old Trafford.

However, after just one day, George and his friend Eric McMordie fled back to Belfast. Matt Busby was understanding and patient, getting George to return within a few weeks. He assigned Henry Gregg to act as 'godfather' and George was given over to the care of Mrs Fullaway, one of Manchester United's 'surrogate mothers' who looked after the domestic needs of United's young talent.

When he arrived in England, 5 feet tall and weighing just 8 stones, it seemed as if George was far too frail for professional football, but come 22 May 1963, his seventeenth birthday, George signed professional forms. By this time Mrs Fullaway's domestic skills had seen him grow to 5 feet 9 inches and he came in at around 10 stones – still a lean, wiry frame but exceptionally strong. Five months later he made his debut on the wing against West Bromwich Albion at Old Trafford. I remember his performance that day being described as 'Bambi on ice'.

BELOW LEFT: **Relaxing in his fashion boutique, June 1967.**

The next season George was a regular. He played 41 League matches, scored ten goals and United pipped Leeds United to the title. Best was a sensation, even in Europe, where Manchester United reached the semi-final of the Fairs Cup. He also won the first of his 37 Northern Ireland caps in April 1964, a win over Wales in Swansea.

Despite his already wild lifestyle, George was exceptionally fit and he rarely missed a match. In 1965/66 he took Europe by storm in the European Cup. In the quarter-final, with a fragile 3-2 first-leg lead, United travelled to the Stadium of Light to play the mighty Benfica, the side that included Europe's top footballer, Eusebio. Busby's team talk urged caution in the first twenty minutes, concentration on keeping the Portuguese champions out. George had obviously not listened to a word, as usual. Within a quarter of an hour he had taken Benfica apart single-handedly, scoring twice and making another. United eventually won the tie 5-1. Benfica had never before been beaten on home soil. Unfortunately Best suffered a knee injury before the semi-final and United went out of the competition.

The following season United won the League title again, Best playing in all 42 matches. He was now 'El Beatle', lionised wherever he went, the owner of boutiques and the darling of the advertising agencies. His picture was everywhere, and his dark good looks were recognised by everyone. He was a genuine

> But George was quite shy, so he didn't really like all the attention. I think that's why he drank, to hide behind a brave face.

superstar. He had made the transition from footballer to recognised celebrity.

But George was quite shy, so he didn't really like all the attention. I think that's why he drank, to hide behind a brave face. He really would have liked to

play and train and go to a disco in the evening to meet new people, but it was always hard in Manchester as you were either a United or a City supporter. It gave him a lot of problems. I remember one night when Bobby Moore and I were with him in a pub called The Brown Bull. When we left and went to drive home, all the tyres on George's car had been slashed. You were either a Red who worshipped at his feet or a Blue who did things like that.

Now in my opinion, had George lived somewhere like Knightsbridge where people just wouldn't know who you were, or if they did they'd turn a blind eye and get on with their lives, then he could have got lost there and lived his own life. When I was a player I always thought this 'bright lights of London' scenario was rubbish, and it was. No one actually lived in central London as it was too expensive. We got paid quite well, but you still lived in the suburbs. If you played for Chelsea you lived in

LEFT: Celebrating the European Cup semi-final victory over Real Madrid, 1968.

> **Maybe the worst thing for George was that the explosive combination of unbelievable talent and good looks gave him a dilemma in life: was he a footballer or a superstar?**

Surrey or Fulham. When I was young, the 'bright lights' were in Manchester or Liverpool. There you lived closer to the ground. It was cheaper, too, and you could go for a good night out. It was definitely the place to be.

George had a part share in a nightclub called Slack Alice. Part of him liked the adoration he got when he walked into the club, another part disliked it immensely. He couldn't really deal with it, this moving into higher social and professional circles at an early age, so he drank to loosen up and lose his shyness, maybe. Whatever the reason, the demon drink got a good hold of him. Of course, he's still battling it today.

In 1968 United at last won the European Cup, at Wembley – against Benfica. Best was crowned European Player of the Year. He'd also scored 28 League goals, the most by any

BELOW: **George scores Manchester United's second goal in their 4-1 European Cup final victory against Benfica at Wembley, 29 May 1968.**

ABOVE: **Playing in the North American Soccer League for the Fort Lauderdale Strikers.**

player in the League, and he'd scored a goal in the European Cup final. He was the most famous player in the world, even though he never had the chance to display his skills on a world stage as Northern Ireland never got to the World Cup finals.

At the age of just 22, he went to see Matt Busby because he felt United needed more young players, that the team should be rebuilt whatever the cost. Busby had always indulged George, but not this time. George's career began to spiral. Just as he had feared, the team began to disintegrate, and by 1974 United had been relegated. Throughout the early seventies he had tried to hold an inferior side together with his great skills, but the glory days were over. Sir Matt retired but stayed on at the club and new managers came and went, unable to reconstruct another great United side.

George Best played his final match for United at QPR on New Year's Day 1974. United lost 3–0. He then moved around, spending time in North America and also at Fulham, living life to the full. The famous story that I love about George dates from this period in his life. His playing days all but over, he's lying on a bed in a hotel suite surrounded by thousands of dollars won in a casino with an ex-Miss World emerging from the shower, her tousled blonde hair and long, sun-tanned legs on show as a Belfast-born waiter enters the room with champagne and says, 'Tell me, George, where did it all start to go wrong for you?'

George still loves his football. He is now a TV pundit for Sky Television, witty and knowledgeable. I feel that had he been given the proper guidance when he was young, the type of advice young players get today, then we might have seen more of George Best's exceptional skills. Instead he had to feel his way and make his own mistakes, and in the end those mistakes cost him and us the chance to enjoy his talents for a good few years longer.

Having said that, George will still go down as one of the all-time greats. He was so incredibly gifted that he only needed to be on top form for a few years, and there is no doubt that he made football a richer sport with his wonderful, exciting, unadulterated talent.

Johan Cruyff

Sublime Player and Coach

JOHAN CRUYFF IS ONE OF THE ALL-TIME GREAT PLAYERS. I'M SURE THAT'S HOW ANYONE WHO WATCHED HIM IN HIS PRIME AND WAS MESMERISED, LIKE I WAS, BY HIS ASTONISHING SKILL WILL REMEMBER HIM.

He was the captain of Holland when that country's football reached a dazzling peak, and he played at that level for eleven exciting years. Johan was a massive influence on the European football scene for over 25 years. The extent of this domination, first as a player with Ajax and Barcelona then as a coach with both clubs, cannot be overemphasised.

As a young boy he grew up in the shadow of the Ajax stadium, living about a quarter of a mile away with his greengrocer father and office cleaner mother. By sheer good fortune his mother worked in the Ajax club offices, and she constantly pestered the management to take her son into their famous youth

> **He would splay passes around and you couldn't get the ball off him. He was like the leader of an orchestra.**

school, which caters not only for youngsters' footballing education but also their academic studies.

So the Ajax youth system embraced Johan from the age of ten, and he worked his way through the various age groups. He progressed with such aplomb that he was able to make his first-team debut at Groningen in November 1964 at the tender age of seventeen. He even scored Ajax's only goal to launch what was to become a quite extraordinary career.

In 1965 he made his debut for the Dutch national Under-18 side, and in 1966 he made his international debut, scoring a goal against Hungary. The coach of that Dutch team was Rinus Michels, and he and Johan would go on to form a very special rela-

tionship that would transform Holland's fortunes.

Johan soon became the finest player in Holland, a supremely gifted striker – although strangely enough, he was not a natural centre-forward. He was more like di Stefano: he could score from deep, and coming in deep he was hard to pick up. He would splay passes around and you couldn't get the ball off him. He was like the leader of an orchestra. He was such a pure footballer, such an elegant person. He was capable of playing in any part of the pitch and had a natural gift for scoring.

BELOW: **Getting a point over for the New York Cosmos, 1978.**

A particular trick of his is still known as 'the Cruyff turn'. To do this, he would come in from the left wing, someone would try to cut it up and he would knock the ball between his legs and behind him and go past the defender. Players used to try to copy him, but no one could do it as well as Johan.

In 1973 Johan was transferred to Barcelona for a world record fee of just under £1 million. Here he joined Michels. He had helped Ajax win six League titles, four cups (the European Cup three times) and

> **Johan was a massive influence on the European football scene for over 25 years. The extent of this domination cannot be overemphasised.**

been voted European Footballer of the Year three times in four years. With these two potent forces in action, together with the aggressive, skilful Johan Neeskens, Barcelona immediately won their first League title for fourteen years.

The Dutch were pioneering the revolutionary 'total football' system at this time, and Johan played

a key role. But if they were the world's best team in the early seventies, then unfortunately they didn't always get the rewards. There are no shortages of examples to illustrate that particular point. For instance, it was West Germany who won the 1974 World Cup after Johan had given Holland the lead in the first minute and the Dutchmen had played the superb, innovative football.

The Dutch were very liberal in their ideals as a society, and their football mirrored that. They were also not slow at coming forward in an argument. In Johan's case, he could also be stubborn. He actually refused to travel to Argentina for the 1978 World Cup after a falling-out with Holland's managerial set-up. The team still made it to the final but lost to the hosts, and rightly felt it was Johan's absence that cost them the title.

That same year he announced his retirement from football, but financial problems persuaded him to join the North American League for three seasons before returning to Ajax to win two more titles. There was another acrimonious departure, and Johan gave the proverbial V-sign to Ajax in 1983 by joining their arch rivals Feyenoord as player/manager, leading them to a Double.

Ajax enticed him back as coach, then he headed off to Barcelona. He had a wonderful coaching career. He arrived at

LEFT: **Cruyff finished his playing career as player/manager at Feyenoord for the 1983/84 season.**

THE VENABLES VERDICT

● *An astonishingly skilful 'Dutch master'.*

● *A massive influence on European football for more than 25 years, both as a player and a coach.*

● *His playing career brought him nine Dutch League titles, six Dutch Cups, one Spanish League title and one Spanish Cup, plus three European Cups and three European Footballer of the Year accolades.*

● *His managerial career brought League titles and Cups in Holland and Spain, two European Cup-Winners' Cups and a European Cup.*

ABOVE: **Cruyff played and managed at the very highest level. His greatest achievement at Barcelona was winning the European Cup in 1992.**

Barcelona after me. I got to the European Cup final and lost on penalties; Johan's team won in 1992, getting their goal in extra time, so he just beat me on that one. Barcelona also won the European Cup-Winners' Cup in 1989 and the Spanish League for four consecutive years from 1991 to 1994. Johan was hailed as a brilliant coach.

I met up with him in Barcelona a few times and we got quite friendly. Recently, I was in Mauritius and he was in the same hotel as me. We often met for an hour in the morning to talk about football. I have always found him very interesting and very positive. He knows exactly what he wants.

He was always a heavy smoker, and in 1996 he suffered a heart attack and retired. I don't think he feels he'll ever go back into coaching. It's a no-win situation, really. I can understand that with what he has achieved, he feels he's done it and doesn't want the stress of doing it any more.

Then again, I think I might have said something similar, then suddenly found myself going through all the stresses and strains of coaching again at Middlesbrough. It's like a drug. When you're in it you sometimes need to get out, when you're out of it you miss it so much you want to get back in again.

Rinus Michels

The World-class Teacher

I T ALWAYS AMAZES ME HOW THE NETHERLANDS, A COUNTRY ABOUT A QUARTER OF THE SIZE OF ENG-LAND, CAN PRODUCE SUCH A QUALITY NATIONAL TEAM WHICH ALWAYS SEEMS TO THRIVE IN EURO-PEAN CHAMPIONSHIPS AND WORLD CUPS AND PRODUCES WORLD-CLASS INDIVIDUALS YEAR AFTER YEAR.

But then the most impressive thing about the Dutch is that they have a capacity for asking tough questions and finding the answers through people like the great Rinus Michels (in England, quite often footballers who have asked questions have been dismissed as nothing more than troublemakers). If you want a constant supply of quality footballers, then that stems from quality teaching. If you have that, you can achieve anything.

Michels is a man for whom I have the highest respect as a teacher of football. After a relatively modest playing career with Ajax, he became one of Europe's leading coaches, revolutionising football as we knew it with his 'total football' theory, executed so brilliantly by Ajax and Holland. These days he is highly respected as one of UEFA's and FIFA's leading coaching consultants.

Holland has always had great teaching methods.

> **The football they produced on the way to that final was so exciting, it really compelled you to watch. It must have made a lot of youngsters want to be footballers.**

In fact, they are second to none. All of us coaches always say we would like to win the World Cup in great style. OK, so Holland reached a World Cup final and lost to West Germany 2-1, but would you rather be remembered as the coach of the team that played a stubborn, strong game or the coach of the team that lost but created dreams for the world's youth and those who watched the game?

Holland surprised everyone in 1974 with Michels' amazing team, playing a beautiful game of football with a new system. The football they produced on the way to that final was so exciting, it really compelled you to watch. It must have made a lot of youngsters want to be footballers. If you had the talent and were hesitating, surely you would have yearned to be part of that new world.

Michels put together a team of creators, not destroyers; he produced the ultimate side, a team that could demolish the opposition inside ten minutes. That Holland side was a magnificent one. I will always admire him for what he did for Holland and the world game.

Before then, Michels of course had a very long

The Dutch have a capacity for asking tough questions and finding the answers.

association with the club he had played for all his career, Ajax. It was he who singled out the young Johan Cruyff as the potential catalyst for his team. Ajax won the League in each of his first three seasons there, doubling their tally since the war. After the third title Ajax at last began to translate their domestic dominance on to the European stage, reaching the 1969 European Cup final in Madrid. Ajax hoped to demonstrate their 'total football' concept to a waiting audience and become Holland's first European champions, but an experienced AC Milan team were too good for them.

While Ajax were trying to conquer Europe, arch rivals Feyenoord won the Dutch League. In 1970 they became Holland's first European Cup winners, beating Celtic in Milan 2-1. But Michels' young team got straight back to business with another League title and followed that with their own European Cup success in 1971. They won it in 1972 and 1973 too – an extraordinary achievement.

But after the 1971 win Michels went to Barcelona. He won the Spanish title with his new club in 1973/74, reaching the European Cup semi-final the following season only to lose to Leeds United. He briefly returned to Ajax as technical director in 1975, but that was a period when PSV were emerging as the top team in Holland, and after just one season in this post he returned to Barcelona and Cruyff, who had moved to Spain in 1973. Michels always did have a special relationship with Cruyff, his 'manager on the field'. Most of his successes at club and international level revolved around Johan.

When he returned, Real Madrid were dominating the Spanish League, although Barcelona did manage a consolation win in the Spanish Cup in 1978. But the Catalans demand more than this, and Michels

RIGHT: **During his spell with FC Köln in the early eighties.**

was replaced. He sought refuge in the USA, coaching the Los Angeles Aztecs for a couple of seasons, Cruyff yet again in his team. Despite this sad end to his time in Spain, when I went to Barcelona they spoke very highly of him. Michels helped the Spanish side become a real force and brought skill and entertainment to the club's football.

After America it was back to Europe and Germany, first with FC Köln then Bayer Leverkusen. But his attentions were turning once again to Dutch football. In 1984 he became technical director of the national side, then the coach, once again, in 1986.

His 'total football' philosophy was still something coaches strove to achieve, but it demanded special footballers who could adapt to the fluid system, which expected players to move into different positions on the field while colleagues covered the vacant areas. It required extremely intelligent players, preferably led by one extraordinary player like Cruyff, someone who could personify the 'total football' concept.

ABOVE: **Rinus coached Holland to the World Cup final in 1974 and then to European Championship glory in 1988.**

Sure enough, in 1988 Michels triumphed in Europe with a team that included talented players like Ruud Gullit, Marco Van Basten, Ronald Köeman, Frank Rijkaard and Arnold Mühren. After an incredible 2-1 victory over the German hosts in the semi-final, Holland easily beat the USSR in the final in Munich, Gullit and Van Basten scoring.

Coaches used to coach and make the players think about the game. Some people would say they created monsters, that they then wanted to run the game with a certain arrogance. Personally, I don't see anything wrong with that. You want the players to end up knowing more than you do as a coach. If you can do that you can achieve something special. I have as much admiration for Michels as a coach as I do for anyone.

You take Brazilian skill for granted, but from a country as small as Holland you don't expect the amazing futuristic football that Michels introduced.

FACT FILE

FULL NAME: *Marinus Jacobus Hendricus Michels*

BORN: *9 February 1928, Amsterdam*

PLAYING CAREER
CLUBS: *Ajax 1946–58*

APPEARANCES/GOALS: *Ajax 269/121*

HONOURS: *Dutch League Champions 1946–47, 1956–57*

INTERNATIONAL: *Holland 5 appearances, 1950–54*

MANAGEMENT CAREER
CLUBS: *JOS Amsterdam (amateurs) 1960–64; AFC Amsterdam (amateurs) 1964–65; Ajax 1965–71; Barcelona 1971–75, 1976–78; Ajax (technical director) 1975–76; Los Angeles Aztecs 1978–80; FC Köln (Germany) 1980–83; Bayer Leverkusen (Germany) 1988–89*

HONOURS: *Dutch League Champions 1966, 1967, 1968, 1970 (with Ajax); Dutch Cup Winners 1967, 1970, 1971 (with Ajax); Spanish League Champions 1974 (with Barcelona); Spanish Cup Winners 1978 (with Barcelona); German Cup Winners 1983 (with FC Köln); European Cup Winners 1970–71 (with Ajax); European Cup Finalists 1968–69 (with Ajax)*

INTERNATIONAL: *Holland national coach 1974, 1986–88, 1990–92; technical director 1984–86*

HONOURS: *World Cup Finalists 1974; European Championship Winners 1988*

Michel Platini

Blue Velvet

IF THERE IS A WORD THAT SUMS UP MICHEL PLATINI, IT HAS TO BE VELVET. I'LL ALWAYS THINK OF HIM AS BEING FOXY, CUNNING AND CLEVER. HE WASN'T A BIG MAN SO THE TEMPTATION FOR HIS OPPONENTS WAS TO BELIEVE THAT THEY COULD OUTSMART HIM PHYSICALLY. BUT THE FRENCHMAN WOULD INVARIABLY GET ONE OVER ON THE OPPOSITION WITH HIS SHREWDNESS AND INTELLIGENCE.

Platini was very smooth, always ahead of everyone. When you speak to a lot of people in the game, it's his name that often crops up as one of the favourite players. You'll hear plenty of talk about Pele, Maradona, Cruyff and di Stefano as huge stars. Michel Platini has to be in that same mould.

When I was managing Barcelona we played against Platini's Juventus in the European Cup. In fact, we knocked them out of the tournament. Twice I travelled to Turin to watch Juventus play in Serie A

> ## Michel's career was tinged with sadness in 1985 when he found himself caught up in the horror of the Heysel disaster.

games with the aim of spotting a way that we could deal with him. By surrounding the Frenchman we managed to contain him very well, to stop him having a free hand, dictating the play, pulling the strings.

Michel Platini was France's first football superstar, and possibly their greatest ever player. Nominally his position was midfield but he was essentially an attacking player blessed with electric speed and supreme ball control. His great strength was his ability to arrive in the penalty area at just the right moment – he was a prolific goalscorer at every level he played. Above all, he was a leader, an intelligent and sensitive man who got the best out of the players around him.

He made his first big impression on the world stage in 1976 when he represented France in the Montreal Olympic Games. Six years later, during the World Cup finals in Spain, he was in dazzling form, inspiring his nation to reach the semi-finals. The opponents were West Germany and despite leading 3-1 in extra time, the French let things slips and were held to a 3-3 draw. The match

BELOW: **Lifting the European Championship trophy, June 1984.**

FACT FILE

FULL NAME: *Michel Platini*

BORN: *21 June 1955, Joeuf, France*

PLAYING CAREER
CLUBS: *AS Nancy-Lorraine (France) 1972–79; AS St Etienne (France) 1979–82; Juventus 1982–87*

APPEARANCES/GOALS: *AS Nancy-Lorraine 175/98; AS St Etienne 107/58; Juventus 147/68*

CAREER TOTAL: *429 appearances/224 goals*

HONOURS: *French League Champions 1980–81 (with St Etienne); French Cup Winners 1977–78 (with Nancy); Italian League Champions 1983–84; Italian Cup Winners 1982–83; European Cup Winners 1984–85; European Cup Finalists 1982–83; European Cup-Winners' Cup Winners 1983–84; European Footballer of the Year 1983, 1984, 1985; World Player of the Year 1984, 1985 (all with Juventus)*

INTERNATIONAL: *France 62 appearances/41 goals, 1979–87*

HONOURS: *European Championship Winner 1984; World Cup Semi-finalist 1982*

MANAGEMENT CAREER
INTERNATIONAL: *French national coach 1987–92*

RIGHT: **Platini brought grace and elegance to the famous black and white stripes of Turin's Juventus. His goalscoring record of almost a goal every other game, from midfield, was remarkable for the Italian game.**

was marred by the disgraceful head-high challenge on the French striker Battiston by the German goalkeeper Schumacher. Battiston was carried off unconscious with no-one knowing the extent of his injury. Although France went on to lose the game's penalty shoot-out, Platini displayed a remarkable ability to remain calm in the face of the tempest, a quality that has earned him as successful and as lucrative a career away from the pitch as on it.

Platini was voted European Footballer of the Year in 1983, and again in both 1984 and 1985. It speaks volumes that only Johan Cruyff and Marco Van Basten have equalled this stunning achievement. In addition to this, Michel was twice voted World Player of the Year, in 1984 and 1985.

In 1984 Juventus followed up their Italian Cup

win of the previous year by clinching the European Cup-Winners' Cup in Basle by beating FC Porto 2-1. For good measure, Juve also won the Italian League title, with Platini as their leading goalscorer. It was a magnificent year for him as he led France to their first European Championship, held on their home soil. Spain were beaten 2-0 in the final in Paris, Platini scoring the all-important first goal during the second half.

Michel's career was tinged with sadness in 1985 when he found himself caught up in the horror of the Heysel disaster. Platini's Juventus were taking on Liverpool in the final of the European Cup at Brussels' Heysel Stadium. The resulting tragedy left its mark on everyone, not least this sensitive Frenchman. His penalty that won the game may have felt hollow, but it defused a very volatile situation that could have led to even greater catastrophe.

He retired from playing in 1987, going on to manage the French national team for five years but

> ## Twice I travelled to Turin to watch Juventus play in Serie A games with the aim of spotting a way that we could deal with him. We managed to stop him having a free hand, dictating the play, pulling the strings.

resigning after a disappointing performance in the 1992 European Championship finals in Sweden. Six years later he was appointed as co-president of the organising committee for the World Cup finals in France in 1998. The tournament was hugely successful, thanks in no small part to Platini's flair and vision, qualities that he had successfully transferred from the playing field to the game's administration.

There was a fairy-tale ending for Platini with an amazing French victory over the might of Brazil. The new French superstar, and successor to Platini's crown, Zinedine Zidane took centre stage and unified the whole of France for one magical moment.

BELOW LEFT: **Feeling the strain as manager of the national side during the 1992 European Championship. Michel resigned shortly after the tournament had finished.**

Steve Archibald

The Talented Individualist

STEVE ARCHIBALD, I WAS TOLD WHEN I WAS AT BARCELONA, COULD BE A PROBLEM, SO BEST NOT TO BUY HIM. I DISREGARDED THE ADVICE AND WILL ALWAYS BE PLEASED I DID. STEVE IS HIS OWN MAN, AND THAT, I AM AFRAID, IS SOMETHING SOME PEOPLE CANNOT COME TO TERMS WITH. BUT IT DOES NOT MAKE HIM A BAD FOOTBALLER AND THAT WAS MY FIRST CONCERN.

My reason for trying to sign him was as a replacement for Diego Maradona whom we had decided should leave for Napoli. The club felt Mexico's Hugo Sanchez was the man to take over the job while I

> **Steve will take any situation and try to make it work for him – and you can't ask for more from any man. As a result, he loved his time in Barcelona.**

thought it should be Archibald. To be frank I didn't see much between them but felt that as this was my first major buy I should be allowed to decide who it was going to be. I spoke to people at Spurs (Steve's club at the time) and the reports about him were excellent – about what he did on the pitch, anyway. The problem, as they saw it, was his attitude: friendly, yes, but a loner. He preferred to walk the pram rather than mix it with the rest of them. What a crime! I never thought that staying at home with the family was a good enough reason to kill a transfer. In fact, some might say that attitude was an asset. I reckoned it this way: if Steve was a loner in England he might as well be a loner in Spain. He came, he conquered, and we have been in touch ever since.

Steve is different, I grant you that. He has a lively mind, is very intelligent, very inquisitive, and he'll

RIGHT: **Bursting through on goal during the 1982 FA Cup final.**

work his socks off for you in whatever project he is involved in. To me, these are qualities you look for in a player when you are a coach.

When you buy in from another country there are so many things to be resolved in your mind as the buyer. In Barcelona's case, and the rule applies to any major club, the player must first have quality. You must believe that what you see in him he will be able to reproduce in a foreign land, most probably under severe pressure without the benefit of being

surrounded by friends, unable to seek them out when an encouraging word is needed. There have been two outstanding examples of this problem in recent years: Mark Hughes, whom I signed for Barca, and Ian Rush, who left Liverpool for Italy. Both of them were superb footballers and really good people – not troublemakers, not rowdies. They had always conducted their lives with a straight bat. Unfortunately they found it very difficult living in a foreign atmosphere. They missed their friends, their game suffered in the process – not disastrously, but enough to be noticed – and they eventually had to repack their bags and go home. I don't blame them for that, it is the way they are, but at the same time everyone would have been a lot happier had they found it easier to integrate.

RIGHT: **Making his contribution to a Scotland victory over the Auld Enemy in May 1985.**

Steve, on the other hand, will take any situation and try to make it work for him – and you can't ask for more from any man. As a result, he loved his time in Barcelona, took to the life, learned to speak Spanish fluently and his game flourished. The fans took to him because he was scoring goals for Barcelona and helped us win the Spanish title, but they also sensed that he was very happy to be among them.

I like it when players question what I am asking them to do. There was no shortage of enquiries from

Steve. Again, some would think 'cheeky so and so', but surely the more a player is aware the better he will be in terms of being able to provide for the team. I have heard stories where Steve apparently stretched the patience of others. The late Jock Stein told me about the time before the World Cup finals in Spain in 1982 when he suggested it would be good to have a straightforward menu at dinner which would suit everybody. It was agreed by all – except Steve. Irritating. He wouldn't have done it to annoy, simply because he knew what he wanted for dinner. I'll add this, though: Jock also told me he had the highest

THE VENABLES VERDICT

• *Very much his own man, something of a loner, but also inquisitive and intelligent.*

• *I signed him from Tottenham for Barcelona in 1984, as a direct replacement for Diego Maradona.*

• *Coped brilliantly with his transfer to Spain, learning the language and adapting to the lifestyle.*

• *Appeared for nine different clubs in a playing career spanning 18 years.*

• *Has won the Scottish and Spanish League titles, the FA Cup and the UEFA Cup.*

FULL NAME: *Steven Archibald*

BORN: *27 September 1956, Glasgow*

PLAYING CAREER

CLUBS: *Clyde 1975–78; Aberdeen 1978–80; Tottenham Hotspur 1980–84; Barcelona 1984–87; Blackburn Rovers 1987–88; Hibernian 1988–90; St Mirren 1990–91; Reading (non-contract) 1991–92; Fulham (non-contract) 1992–93*

APPEARANCES/GOALS:

	League	FA Cup	FL Cup	European
Clyde	*65/7*			
Aberdeen	*76/29*	*10/11*	*18/6*	*6/0*
Tottenham Hotspur	*131/58*	*17(1)/5*	*18/7*	*22/8*
FC Barcelona	*97/42*			
Blackburn Rovers	*20/6*	*1/0*		
Hibernian	*44/15*			
St Mirren	*16/2*			
Reading	*2/0*			
Fulham	*2/0*			

CAREER TOTAL: *545(1) appearances/196 goals*

HONOURS: *FA Cup Winners 1981, 1982 (with Tottenham Hotspur); Scottish League Champions 1979–80 (with Aberdeen); Scottish League runners-up 1977–78 (with Aberdeen); Scottish League Cup Finalists 1978–79, 1979–80 (with Aberdeen); Scottish Second Division Champions 1977–78 (with Clyde); Spanish League Champions 1984–85 (with Barcelona); European Cup Finalists 1985–86 (with Barcelona); UEFA Cup Winners 1983–84 (with Tottenham Hotspur)*

INTERNATIONAL: *Scotland 27 appearances/4 goals, 1980–86*

MANAGEMENT CAREER

CLUBS: *East Fife 1995–96*

HONOURS: *promoted to First Division 1995–96 (with East Fife)*

> Steve has a lively mind, is very intelligent, very inquisitive, and he'll work his socks off for you in whatever project he is involved in.

ABOVE: **With Alan Harris and me on the pitch at the Camp Nou, freshly signed from Spurs, July 1984.**

possible regard for Steve Archibald as a player.

We only had one falling-out and that was when he turned up for training wearing an earring. There are some things I will accept, others I am less tolerant about. Players and earrings do not go together. I called him in and asked him why he was wearing it. 'What?' he replied. 'The earring,' I said. 'I want to. Anyway, it cost me a thousand pounds.' 'If you had this urge to wear a tiara during a match, would that be all right? I don't want to see you wearing that again on club duty, OK?' I told him. 'You're right,' he then said, starting to laugh.

And I was quite satisfied that the problem was solved. He was the type who would challenge you but would hold his hands up if you countered his argument well – except on this occasion. At the next session I saw him sneak in and imagined I'd seen a little flash of jewellery about his ear. I called him over and ordered him to remove the earring, to which he replied that it had just fallen off. We got down on our hands and knees and looked for it. I gave up after a minute or two, and only recently did I learn that Steve never did find that earring. It is still there, buried somewhere on the Barcelona training ground. I told him it served him right.

Bryan Robson

Captain Marvel

BRYAN ROBSON WAS A COLOSSUS AS A PLAYER, A ONCE-IN-A-GENERATION FIND, A PLAYER SO IMMENSELY TALENTED HE WOULD HAVE BEEN OUTSTANDING IN ANY TEAM, ANYWHERE, ANYTIME.

I've been an admirer since I first came across him as a member of the England Under-21 side when I was coach with Dave Sexton in the eighties. When I took over as England manager he was one of the first names on my team sheet. In return, when he hit a bit of a wall at Middlesbrough, he called on me and I was only too happy to help.

Unfortunately he has left the club and there is real sadness in that. I hope he sees it as further challenge and finds himself another club good enough to deserve him. He's certainly learned enough from his

> ## Men like Robson only appear very rarely and when they do you can only thank the gods for them.

experiences at the Riverside to emerge as a highly successful manager.

Men like Robson only appear very rarely and when they do you can only thank the gods for them. When I sat down to analyse what he has done, what he has meant to both club and country as player, manager and coach, I quickly realised why he was called Captain Marvel.

He was skilful, highly talented and very brave. He was reckless and that was why his career was dominated by injury and lay-offs. There would be constant updates on his fitness and whether or not he would be ready for such and such a match. But that was Robbo and you were never going to change the way he threw himself so completely into a match.

If there was a flaw in his game, that was it. He was reckless. He didn't just go into a tackle, he strained every sinew to try to stop an opponent and reach the ball. While others were a little more cautious, Bryan would stretch out his leg and it would too often take the full impact of his opponent's own powerful challenge. The result was obvious – another injury, another spell of treatment, another series of matches missed.

LEFT: **A shoulder injury forces Bryan to leave the field during England's group match against Morocco at the 1986 Mexico World Cup.**

Maybe it couldn't have been any other way; it was like that from the very beginning with Bryan and you just had to accept it. In truth, only a foolish manager/coach wouldn't have been prepared to live with Robbo for the great days when he was fit and playing like a dream. He was a midfielder who

scored goals. The whole pitch was his domain. With him in your side you had a chance. If there was a player I'd take into battle with me, Bryan Robson would be my choice and I am certain he'd be the choice of everyone who saw him play and knew the strength of his character.

When you consider people like Bryan you tend to cut them off from real life, to see them only as a personality. But over the years I have had lots of time to talk and discuss things with him, not just football. It's important to know that not only is Bryan a foot-

ball man of high stature, hugely respected throughout the world game, but a decent man who generally copes with the pressures which are presumably invisible to the rest of us.

It hurt me a lot when he was booed by a section of the crowd in Middlesbrough's last match of the 2000/01 season. I said at the time and I repeat

If there was a player I'd take into battle with me, Bryan Robson would be my choice.

BELOW: **Raw emotion as Bryan and Gary Lineker celebrate Robbo's goal against Holland in the 1988 European Championship.**

it now: there is no way he deserved that. The fans are entitled to their opinion but they must have realised the circumstances were difficult enough for Bryan, surely remembered what he has done for Boro. They should have given him their thanks, not a mouthful of abuse. You know, if you take time to consider the situation at Middlesbrough before Bryan arrived, the

well. No-one could ever accuse Bryan of taking it easy, either in the days when he 'ran' matches on the pitch, or when he had to get others to do what he wanted on the field.

As I've said, I first came into contact with Bryan when he was in the national Under-21 team. His club side was West Brom. There was never any doubt about his progression to the senior squad. It was a case of inevitable promotion for a young man who knew no fear and would go on to join Manchester United and be their captain as well as England's.

That reckless streak did cost him. His career would have been different but no less praiseworthy had he been able to control that one side of his nature. Did it overlap into his everyday life? I honestly don't know. With Bryan that old phrase applies – what you see is what you get. I think his former boss Sir Alex Ferguson summed him up pretty well when he said, 'Bryan Robson never sensed danger and that's what made him such a formidable opponent. He was a lion of a player, born with an unflinching "have a go" instinct.' Robbo never lost that; he never allowed terrible injury to curb his challenges, undermine his confidence or destroy his resolve. You would suppose a man who has broken, fractured or dislocated something like

ABOVE LEFT: **Robbo always had a keen eye for goal, as 144 career strikes would confirm. Not bad from midfield!**

club was struggling. Since Steve Gibson has taken over as owner/chairman he has given Boro a wonderful modern stadium, convinced Bryan to join him, put up the necessary funds, and transformed them from being one of football's unconsidered teams to a club of international repute.

The money from Steve Gibson was vital but even with unlimited cash – and Robbo never had that – it was Bryan's stature in the game worldwide that attracted top names to Teesside. Can you imagine Juninho or Ravanelli or Boksic or Karembeu turning up in the North-east solely for the money? Robbo was the catch.

I thought he made the difficult transition from top-class, high-profile player to manager superbly

24 bones in his body would hold back a little from making it 25 – but he didn't.

What of his record? He played for Washington and Chester-le-Street Schoolboys before joining West Brom in September 1972, signing pro forms two years later and making his senior debut in April 1975. In his first season in the First Division he broke his leg on three occasions. Can you imagine how that alone would have done for some? Not Bryan. Ron

ABOVE: **Leading out Manchester United for the very last time, May 1994.**

Atkinson was his manager at the time and when Big Ron was appointed boss at Old Trafford in 1981, Robbo joined him a little later for £1.5 million, then a British transfer record.

The domestic honours started to pile up, the first being an FA Cup winners medal after a Wembley replay against Brighton. He had already been selected for England, had played in the 1982 World Cup and scored twice in the opening game against France in what was to be a 3-1 victory under Ron Greenwood. Bryan's opening goal came inside the

> ## I hope Bryan's future will be the brilliant one he deserves. Many others will be wishing the same.

first minute – in 27 seconds to be exact – then the second fastest strike in the World Cup finals. It is still the fastest by an Englishman. Robbo is also the second fastest England scorer with his goal against Yugoslavia in 1989, timed at 38 seconds.

Spain was an injury-free World Cup for Bryan but he was to suffer badly with physical problems in the next two – Mexico 1986 and Italy 1990. He was there for both and gave it everything until his body let him down.

Robbo was the man I wanted for England. He had just finished playing and I believed we needed a link between the players and the management, someone nearer their age group who would see things their way. Robbo was the man. He was not only highly respected and greatly liked, he had been

through it all, knew where the problems were and how they could best be dealt with. He was an immediate success, a vital part of my coaching team. I valued his input and his friendship. My only regret is we didn't win the European Championship in 1996, which we should have done.

Bryan is a great lad. When I joined him at Middlesbrough I guess he was battle weary. Bobby Keetch used to say to me, 'That which doesn't destroy you completely will only make you stronger.' I hope Bryan's future will be the brilliant one he deserves. He can be assured many others will be wishing the same for one of the game's most inspiring figures.

BELOW LEFT: **Robbo returns to Old Trafford as boss of Middlesbrough, November 2000.**

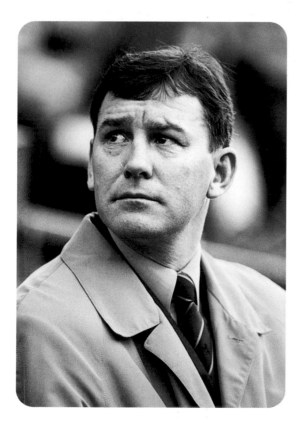

FACT FILE

FULL NAME: *Bryan Robson, OBE*

BORN: *11 January 1957, Witton Gilbert, Chester-le-Street, Co. Durham*

PLAYING CAREER
CLUBS: *West Bromwich Albion 1974–81; Manchester United 1981–94; Middlesbrough (player/manager) 1994–97*

APPEARANCES/GOALS:

	League	FA Cup	FL Cup	European
WBA	194(4)/39	10(2)/2	17(1)/2	12/3
Manchester United	326(19)/74	33(2)/10	49(1)/5	26(1)/8
Middlesbrough	23(2)/1	1/0	1/0	

CAREER TOTAL: *692(32) appearances/144 goals*

HONOURS: *Premier League Champions 1992–93, 1993–94; First Division runners-up 1987–88, 1991–92 (all with Manchester United); First Division Champions 1994–95 (with Middlesbrough); FA Cup Winners 1983, 1985 and 1990; League Cup Finalists 1990–91; European Cup-Winners' Cup 1990–91 (all with Manchester United); promoted from Second Division 1975–76 (with WBA)*

INTERNATIONAL: *England 90 appearances/26 goals, 1980–92; captain on 65 occasions*

MANAGEMENT CAREER
CLUBS: *Middlesbrough 1994–2001*

HONOURS: *First Division Champions 1994–95; First Division runners-up 1997–98; FA Cup Finalists 1997; League Cup Finalists 1996–97, 1997–98 (all with Middlesbrough)*

Bernd Schuster

Maverick Talent

I FIRST SAW BERND SCHUSTER PLAY FOR WEST GERMANY IN THE EUROPEAN CHAMPIONSHIP IN 1980. HE WAS ONLY TWENTY YEARS OF AGE AT THE TIME YET HE WAS VOTED THE PLAYER OF THE TOURNAMENT. I THOUGHT HIS WAS ONE OF THE MOST IMPRESSIVE MIDFIELD DISPLAYS I'D SEEN, THE BEST PASSING SINCE JOHNNY HAYNES. I COULDN'T GET OVER HOW GOOD THIS PLAYER WAS.

I had dinner around about this time with Ron Greenwood and the German manager of the time, Juup Derwald. Derwald said, 'This boy is going to be the next Franz Beckenbauer.'

Bernd made his Bundesliga debut with FC Köln, having spent his formative years with clubs in his native Augsburg, and looked to have the world at his feet. But by the time I joined Bernd at Barcelona in May 1984 his international career was already coming to an end. In fact, he had refused to play for West Germany again. I remember Franz Beckenbauer ringing me several times in Mexico when I was out

> **We'd just finished training and all the players were stark naked in the showers and getting changed when in through the door walked Mrs Schuster. She marched right across the dressing room without blinking.**

there watching a World Cup warm-up tournament featuring England, Italy, West Germany and Mexico. Franz was desperately trying to get Bernd back in the national side.

In fact, he rang me so many times it became something of a joke. The Tannoy would go and over would come the message: 'Franz Beckenbauer for Terry Venables'. I'd be thinking, 'Not again! What more can I say to him?' It put me in mind of that

great Frank Sinatra story. A punter saw Sinatra in a restaurant, went over to him and said, 'I'm dining with a beautiful girl tonight and I really want to make a good impression. It would mean a lot to me if she thought I had great connections. Do you think you could come over to our table and just say hi to me?' Sinatra agreed. The girl arrived, they had dinner, and towards the end Sinatra came over and said, 'Hey, Tony, how ya doin'? You gonna introduce me to your beautiful companion?' To which Tony replied, 'Don't disturb me now, Frank, can't you see I'm busy?' Well, it was like that with Franz. Everyone entered into the joke. Except Bernd, who still refused to play.

He may not have been good for Franz, but he was great for me. Our relationship was good. In my first season at Barcelona he played in 32 matches, scored 11 goals and we won the League. The fans loved him. He was exactly their kind of player, committed and talented. They've always loved a good player there. He had just returned from injury when I arrived. He had suffered two broken legs in his career and had a bit of a limp, but he still maintained incredible form.

He was playing well the next season too, and the team was doing well, particularly in the European Cup. Then suddenly, halfway through that season, he said he wanted to leave. I was taken aback and asked him why. He said it was because he'd been at the club long enough and wanted a change. So I struck a deal with him: we were having a good run in the

FULL NAME:: *Bernd Schuster*

BORN: *22 December 1959, Augsburg, Germany*

PLAYING CAREER
CLUBS: *SV Hammerschmiede Augsburg 1971-76; FC Augsburg 1976-78; FC Köln 1978-80; Barcelona 1980-88; Real Madrid 1988-90; Atletico Madrid 1990-93; Bayer Leverkusen 1993-95; UNAM Mexico City 1996-97*

APPEARANCES/GOALS: *FC Köln 61/10; FC Barcelona 295/103; Real Madrid 61/13; Atletico Madrid 85/11; Bayer Leverkusen 59/8; UNAM Mexico City 9/0*

CAREER TOTAL: *570 appearances/145 goals*

HONOURS: *Spanish League Champions 1984-85 (with Barcelona); 1988-89, 1989-90 (with Real Madrid); Spanish Cup Winners 1981, 1982, 1988 (with Barcelona), 1989 (with Real Madrid), 1991, 1992 (with Atletico Madrid); Spanish League Cup Winners 1983, 1986 (with Barcelona); Spanish Super Cup Winners 1989 (with Real Madrid); European Cup Finalists 1985-86 (with Barcelona); European Cup-Winners' Cup Winners 1981-82 (squad member with Barcelona)*

INTERNATIONAL: *West Germany 21 appearances/4 goals, 1979-84*

HONOURS: *European Championship Winners 1980*

COACHING CAREER: *SC Fortuna Köln 1997-98; FC Köln 1998-99; currently with coaching staff at Barcelona*

> I thought his was one of the most impressive midfield displays I'd seen, the best passing since Johnny Haynes. I couldn't get over how good this player was.

have a bit of a rant and rave at my talking so directly like that. Some players don't like you interfering in their personal lives, but he was fine about her coming in to see me. So in she came, and it was really funny.

When you go into the dressing room at Barcelona there's a little office on the left, which was mine. The dressing room attached to it is so huge you could land Concorde in it. In the corner is a door that comes in from the gymnasium, which functions as a sort of back entrance in and out for the players. We'd just finished training and all the players were stark naked in the showers and getting changed when in through that door walked Mrs Schuster. She marched right across the dressing room without blinking (although she did have a little look around) and came straight over to me. Thankfully, I was fully dressed in my football kit.

I asked her if she was all right and we went and had a chat. We ended up talking for about an hour, and after I'd repeated my promise that I'd make sure the President released him, she agreed to let Bernd stay at the club until the end of the season. I think she'd just got fed up with the media pressure and all the things that were being written about him.

We continued to do well in the European Cup. We beat Juventus, winning 1-0 at home and Archibald scoring a crucial equaliser when we were losing 1-0 away. Then we played Gothenburg. We lost 3-0 in Sweden, won 3-0 at home and got through on penalties. So it was Steaua Bucharest in the final in Seville. It was a really boring game. Bernd

OPPOSITE: **Bernd's passing displays for West Germany in the 1980 European Championship were absolutely remarkable for one so young.**

European Cup, so I asked him to stay until the end of the season and then I promised I would get the President to let him go. He agreed and off he went.

Now everyone had told me that Bernd was a bit strange, that he was dominated by his wife. She had modelled for German magazines, which left him wide open to the sort of banter you'd expect in the dressing room – banter he didn't cope with very well. So the next morning he came back to my office and knocked on my door. 'I still want to leave,' he said. 'What's happened, Bernd? All you've done is gone home. It must be your wife who's persuaded you to change your mind. There's no point in talking to you, then. Send your wife in tomorrow and I'll have a chat to her.'

He agreed, which surprised me. I thought he'd

stopped working for some reason, but he was one of my penalty takers so I was determined to keep him on the way the game was going. Then there was a period when the Romanians began to push forward and look dangerous, and I was convinced we would not get to penalties. So I subbed him – he really wasn't doing his job properly – the game went to penalties and we lost 2-0.

To cap it all, when I got back into the dressing room, Bernd had vanished. Before the game I had told the players that every one of them had to stay at the stadium in case there were drug tests. If the authorities call a player and he's not there, they can impose penalties on the club. But Bernd was

> The fans loved him. He was exactly their kind of player, committed and talented. They've always loved a good player there.

nowhere to be seen. Fortunately, he didn't get chosen for a drug test, but had he been Barcelona could have got banned from European competition. It was a very serious thing to have done, and I was absolutely furious with him, for the way he'd played and for the way he'd put the club in jeopardy after the game. So the next season I didn't recommend to the President that Bernd should be allowed to leave, he had to stay and I didn't play him once. He trained, but he never played. That was his punishment.

We've spoken since, at the centenary celebrations at Barcelona. All the players and staff met up and it was great. We had a chat and there were no hard feelings, and I have to say that overall Bernd was good for the club. What he did could have had serious consequences, and a player can't do things like that, but I liked the guy all the same and he's been successful in his playing career, as a coach in Germany, and now he's on the coaching staff at the Camp Nou.

OPPOSITE: **Bernd had seven good years in the famous colours of FC Barcelona.**

BELOW: **Directing operations from the touch-line while manager at FC Köln, March 1999.**

Diego Maradona

The Greatest on Earth

DIEGO MARADONA AND I MET AND TALKED, BUT WE NEVER WORKED TOGETHER. OUR PROFESSIONAL RELATIONSHIP THEREFORE DIDN'T LAST LONG ENOUGH FOR ME TO LEARN IF ALL THE STORIES ABOUT HIM DOING THE ROUNDS AT BARCELONA WERE TRUE OR JUST FANTASY.

What I did find out during my short spell with him confirmed what a delight he was to be with. I already knew he was a talent without measure. He was the sort who lit up the dressing room; up front, gregarious, always talking, full of banter. Contrary to many of the stories told about him, the other players loved him. There was this perception that Diego was aloof, a real prima donna, an uncontrollable big head. It

> **The pressures imposed on him, maybe even the pressures he placed on himself, must have been intense enough to drive any man to the very edge of madness.**

just wasn't true, though of course he had his problems, some of which – too many of which – have made for lurid headlines about drug abuse, failing health and a deteriorating state of mind.

It wasn't true either that I was the one who wanted rid of him at Barcelona. It was quite the reverse. Nothing would have given me greater satisfaction than to work closely with a player who unarguably was the greatest footballer on earth, the biggest star of his generation, someone whose talent was so extraordinary he is instantly recognisable in households in every continent. Why would I want to give a player like that away?

When I arrived in Barcelona I had prepared myself by studying their squad, and I was looking forward to meeting Diego. But almost as soon as I

arrived I was told to decide whether he was to be sold or retained. My official reply was: why not find me something difficult to start off with? It was clear he wanted out because of the disgraceful punishment he had had to withstand on Spanish pitches. The club, I have to say, weren't averse to

BELOW: **The sheer joy of another beautiful Maradona goal.**

agreeing to a transfer. He was being kicked out of Spain, literally. The tackling he had had to suffer could justifiably be described as criminal. The defender they called the Butcher of Bilbao, Andoni Goicoechea, nearly finished him off with one challenge which left Diego hospitalised and requiring three steel pins in his leg. It was a bad situation for him, one I was being asked to resolve. For me, the decision depended on whom I could bring in: I wanted Steve Archibald, the club directors thought the Mexican Hugo Sanchez would be ideal. Both players would have given me exactly what I wanted, but I won the argument – I had to – and Archibald it was, to everyone's surprise.

I arranged a deal for Diego with Napoli, who had come in for him and agreed a £6.9 million world

There will be those who argue that all Diego's problems were self-inflicted. Shame on them.

record transfer fee. Maradona allegedly had a retinue of 40 people with him in Barcelona, all of them, we were told, living off him and signing for food, clothes, drink – everything on his bill, everything paid for by his talent. It wasn't a healthy situation, and he needed and deserved help. I tried to deal with this situation and left him in good order with money in the bank and the problem of running out of cash solved – temporarily, at least.

There will be those who argue that all Diego's problems were self-inflicted. Shame on them. They were the result in the main of his generosity. It was his openness, I suspect, his determination to be looked on as just an ordinary man, which sadly made him a victim. Diego had the world at his feet; then, ironically, he miskicked the ball. It is hard to understand what sustains a celebrity like Diego unless you have had the opportunity to sit down and talk with him for a few days. Very few were afforded that singular honour, but you'd soon realise how much he craved a simple, normal life. It was denied him, and in that respect there is a strong similarity

between Diego and someone like Paul Gascoigne. I am not comparing them, but they both possessed outstanding talents with great characters. Although both had what you might call 'reputations', were labelled troublemakers and were seemingly always trying to cope with difficult personal problems, they were still loved by their team-mates, the people who really knew them. The reason for that is that both were givers. They wanted to be part of whatever

BELOW: **Beautifully balanced, the little maestro glides past Peter Beardsley during Argentina's controversial quarter-final victory in the 1986 Mexico World Cup.**

was going on, they wanted to be included. They wanted to contribute.

I've said it before, and I'll say it again here: I never had any lasting problem with either Paul or Diego. Maybe such a situation would have developed with the Argentinian, but I have no reason to think so. I was genuinely saddened, shocked even, to watch his deterioration and, at times, humiliation over the years. How much truth there is in the stories that have surfaced I couldn't say. The seedier aspects we certainly could have done without knowing. But it is obvious he has gone from the very top, which is where he was when he left Barcelona, to rock-bottom.

Diego's life story is a remarkable one, some of which I learned from him, some from the likes of Cesar Luis Menotti, the former Argentina and Barcelona coach who was among the first to realise the potential of the stocky little player from the poorest of backgrounds in Buenos Aires, and some of it from the headlines he created in Italy and then in the USA during the 1994 World Cup finals when he was banned after testing positive for a cocktail of drugs (we were told). He was one of eight children in a family which literally struggled to survive. When he was seven he made extra money for them by juggling oranges with his feet in a variety show. He played organised football with a team called Estrella Roja,

RIGHT: **Another dramatic tumble in the penalty area.**

There is a strong similarity between Diego and someone like Paul Gascoigne. They both possessed outstanding talents with great characters.

then set up his own side with some friends and they called themselves 'the little onions'. They were so good that Argentinos Juniors signed them on, all of them, and used them as one of their junior sides.

The bald statistics of his career confirm the prodigious talent and remarkable skills of this uneducated youngster. He made his pro debut as a fifteen-year-old in 1976 and his international debut four months later against Hungary. The rest, as they say, we all know. He was red-carded in the 1982 World Cup in Spain when he eventually cracked after being kicked mercilessly during the second-phase matches against Brazil and Italy. It didn't put him off Spain, however, and he went off to join Barcelona for a record £4.2 million. I helped him move to Italy after that, as I explained, and that should have been good recovery time for him. It seemed he had managed to settle down in Serie A, but despite helping Napoli win two championships in seven years the crowd began slowly to turn against him and it all went dreadfully wrong.

LEFT: **Anyone who witnessed it will never forget this goal celebration from the 1994 World Cup finals in the USA.**

Things came to a head after Argentina's World Cup final defeat against Germany in Rome in 1990. What followed was a series of scandals related to a court case which detailed his connections with drugs and prostitution. He tested positive for cocaine and was banned from the game for fifteen months. For some in England, these revelations came as no surprise, for Diego Maradona remained the little cheat who scored the 'Hand of God' goal in Mexico City's Azteca Stadium, the goal that dumped Bobby Robson and his team out of the 1986 World Cup. Yes, he fisted the ball away from Peter Shilton's

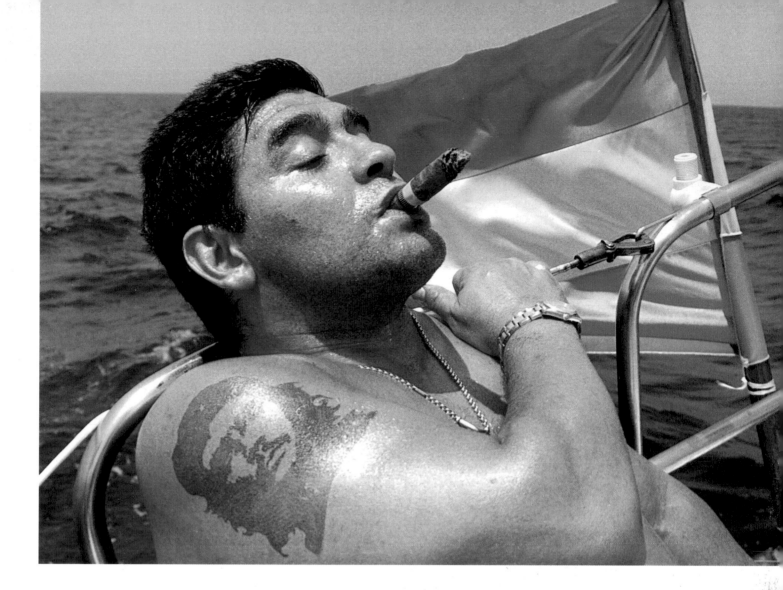

challenge to score. Yes, it was outrageous, and the referee did nothing about it. But in any game there will always be times when illegal moves pay off, and what we also seem to conveniently forget in the mists of time is the perfectly legal goal he did score against us – arguably one of the greatest goals ever witnessed in the finals of the world's greatest football event.

You can't legislate for talents as dazzling as Diego Maradona's, you can only give them space to breathe, then marvel at what they can produce. I don't think there is a bad bone in his body, not one. The pressures imposed on him, maybe even the pressures he placed on himself, must have been intense enough to drive any man to the very edge of madness. I hope Diego can find a corner to turn, to some place where there is sanctuary and peace and contentment for him and the family I know he adores. Someone who has given so much to so many shouldn't be asked to suffer as he has suffered. It's not right.

FACT FILE

FULL NAME: *Diego Armando Maradona*

BORN: *30 October 1960, Lanus, Buenos Aires*

PLAYING CAREER
CLUBS: *Argentinos Juniors (Argentina) 1976–81; Boca Juniors (Argentina) 1981–82, 1994–95; Barcelona 1982–84; Napoli (Italy) 1984–91, Sevilla (Spain) 1992–93; Newell's Old Boys (Argentina) 1993–94*

APPEARANCES/GOALS: *Argentinos Juniors 166/116; Boca Juniors 71/35; Barcelona 58/38; Napoli 259/115; Sevilla 29/7; Newell's Old Boys 16/6*

CAREER TOTAL: *599 appearances/317 goals*

HONOURS: *Argentinian Championship 1981 (with Boca Juniors); Italian League Championship 1987, 1990 (with Napoli); Spanish Cup Winners 1983 (with Barcelona); Italian Cup Winners 1987 (with Napoli); UEFA Cup Winners 1987 (with Napoli); World Footballer of the Year 1986; South American Footballer of the Year 1979, 1980*

INTERNATIONAL: *Argentina 90 appearances/34 goals, 1977–94*

HONOURS: *World Cup Winner 1986; World Cup Finalist 1990*

Gary Lineker

Goalscoring Specialist

THERE WAS NOTHING MYSTERIOUS ABOUT GARY LINEKER'S GOALSCORING SUCCESS — HE WAS SIMPLY SMARTER THAN THE AVERAGE DEFENDER.

I've known him for a long time – we were both part of the Barcelona experience when I signed him from Everton in a £5.7 million deal – and in that time I've heard him dismiss his own ability as a footballer, say-

> **When I say Gary used his brain to score goals, I mean there has been no-one sharper or better equipped to spot and exploit a defender's weakness.**

ing that he didn't have a thimbleful of the talent of such-and-such a player. I don't doubt he meant it. For all his success, Gary's feet always remained on the ground. He had a perspective on life in general which gave football its place of importance, but it didn't come before his family.

He may not have possessed the skills of some players, but Gary was a specialist, and his speciality was scoring goals. Only one Englishman, Sir Bobby Charlton, has a better record for England. Bobby hit 49, one more than Gary managed during a career in which his remarkable finishing saved England from Monterrey in Mexico to Poznan in Poland.

When I say Gary used his brain to score goals, I mean there has been no-one sharper

LEFT: **Displaying that trademark turn of pace for Everton in the 1986 FA Cup final.**

or better equipped to spot and exploit a defender's weakness. I am attributing a lot to him that he will say has to do with being in the right place at the right time. But believe me, even if it was so simple, it would still be a talent all of its own. I don't know if you can put the whole package Gary offered down to pure natural ability, but for sure no modern striker from these islands has come close to him in his prime. That, as it happens, goes for a lot of defenders he faced too.

Gary's pace was a considerable weapon; one-on-one, he'd come first nine times out of ten. He could accelerate away from a defender and be gone in a flash. He had this uncanny knack of knowing where there would be most space for him to operate in, and that was vital. His runs were so, so clever. Gary was

a box player who rarely hit the ball over the bar. I used to spend a lot of time telling the players there was nothing in it for them if they shot over or wide. I would rather see a soft shot on target than a power shot over the top because there was always a chance for a soft shot to stay in play, maybe come back to you or to someone who could do something with it. Gary reduced the number of wasted chances in front of goal, or rather was very rarely careless like that.

He made goalscoring look easy when he converted his classic strikes. I remember in particular one of his goals at Barcelona. It was between him and the keeper, and unusually he was running from a long way out. He stayed cool when others might have panicked, and waited until the very last second to make his move, scooping the ball at pace over the keeper. It looked so simple, yet it could not have been more difficult.

You couldn't help but like him and his family. He was a very warm person, had plenty to say, was easy to talk to and funny. He always listened but was fairly fixed on his ideas and was never a great one for

practising. He enjoyed his football but it was a bread-winning occupation and he certainly wasn't the type to stay behind to work. Considering what a pleasant personality he has, it doesn't surprise me that he is successful in the media. It was what he always intended doing when his playing career ended. The one thing he had no interest in being was a coach.

Gary had a logical view of the game and he was his equable self win or lose. That can be hard for some to accept, and I can think of at least one match after which he

BELOW: **Basking in the glory of Tottenham's 1991 FA Cup final victory over Nottingham Forest.**

> He had a perspective on life in general which gave football its place of importance, but it didn't come before his family.

THE VENABLES VERDICT

- *A clinical finisher, particularly when one-on-one with the goalkeeper. Always stayed cool.*

- *Made goalscoring look easy. Smarter than the defenders who opposed him. A great box player.*

- *His feet always remained on the ground. Had a healthy sense of perspective.*

- *From 80 international appearances, scored an amazing 48 goals, just one behind Bobby Charlton's all-time record.*

- *Twice voted Footballer of the Year, in 1986 with Everton and in 1992 with Tottenham Hotspur.*

Just one of Gary's 48 goals for his country.

annoyed everyone by seemingly treating a bad result lightly. No one had moved in the dressing room that day; the mood was black. But there was Gary, I won't say whistling a merry tune, but walking out shouting, 'Come on lads, it was only a game!'

He and his wife went through hell when their baby son was diagnosed as having leukaemia. When I heard I went straight round to his house. It was a very emotional time for them. I am not the crying type, but I felt I wanted to cuddle him. In truth, I didn't know what to say. Here I was – a coach, a teacher, a leader. I felt I should have been leading at that moment but I didn't know how to deal with the situation. He seemed lost, I was mortified. Thankfully everything turned out well, but the experience must have had an effect on his attitude to life and the game of football. When the battle was won it would have been uplifting; it would have placed things nicely in perspective. When you look at life that way, football really is 'only a game'.

FACT FILE

FULL NAME: *Gary Winston Lineker*

BORN: *30 November 1960, Leicester*

PLAYING CAREER
CLUBS: *Leicester City 1979–85; Everton 1985–86; Barcelona 1986–89; Tottenham Hotspur 1989–92; Nagoya Grampus Eight (Japan) 1992–93*

APPEARANCES/GOALS:

	League	FA Cup	FL Cup	European
Leicester City	187(7)/95	13/5	9/2	
Everton	41/30	6/5	5/3	5/2
FC Barcelona	99/44			
Tottenham Hotspur	105/67	9/3	17/8	9/2

CAREER TOTAL: *505(7) appearances/266 goals*

HONOURS: *First Division runners-up 1985–86 (with Everton); FA Cup Winners 1991 (with Tottenham Hotspur); FA Cup Finalists 1986 (with Everton); Spanish Cup Winners 1990 (with Barcelona); European Cup-Winners' Cup Winners 1988–89 (with Barcelona); Footballer of the Year 1986 (with Everton), 1992 (with Tottenham Hotspur); PFA Player of the Year 1986 (with Everton)*

INTERNATIONAL: *England 80 appearances/48 goals, 1984–92*

Marco Van Basten

The Complete Striker

MARCO VAN BASTEN'S EARLY RETIREMENT THROUGH INJURY WAS A TRAGEDY. THE DUTCHMAN WAS STILL IN HIS TWENTIES. WHEN YOU THINK ABOUT IT, MOST OF THE GAME'S GREAT PLAYERS HAVE HAD LONG CAREERS. POOR MARCO WAS VERY UNFORTUNATE.

He was part of the Holy Trinity of Rijkaard, Gullit and Van Basten but in my opinion Marco was the best. He looked like a typical Dutch player – tall, lean and athletic. The goal he scored against the USSR in the 1988 European Championship final was incredible; one of the all-time great strikes.

Van Basten was the outstanding centre-forward in European football throughout the eighties and into the nineties until ankle injury robbed the world of one of its star players. He was the complete striker, as capable of cracking in spectacular goals from all angles as of scoring the 'bread and butter' tap-ins so beloved of the natural predator.

> It was a long cross from the left that he met with a fantastic, athletic volley from the narrowest of angles.

Marco was a product of the famed Ajax youth system and he made his debut for the Amsterdam club in the 1981/82 season, which brought them yet another League title. Two seasons later Van Basten topped the Dutch League scoring charts with 28 goals from 26 appearances, although rivals Feyenoord would 'steal' the championship from Ajax, masterminded as they were by player/manager Johan Cruyff.

Van Basten made his first international appearance for Holland in September 1983 against Iceland at Groningen in a European Championship qualifier. His first international goal, two weeks later against Belgium in Brussels, forced a 1-1 draw.

In the 1985/86 season the Dutchman registered his best ever scoring total with 37 goals in 26 matches. The tally not only made him his country's top scorer but also won him the coveted European Golden Boot.

Soon he was on his way to Italy, signed by AC Milan for £1.5 million, a sum that was terrific value at the time (1987). The following summer was an excellent one for Van Basten as Holland won the European Championship.

BELOW: **That wonder volley against the USSR that clinched Holland's victory in the 1988 European Championship final in Munich.**

He was part of the Holy Trinity of Rijkaard, Gullit and Van Basten but in my opinion Marco was the best.

His five goals from five appearances included a hat-trick against England. Later that year he was voted European Footballer of the Year as well as World Player of the Year.

At the conclusion of that season AC Milan were crowned European Cup champions as they beat Romanian side Steaua Bucharest 4-0, with Gullit and Van Basten scoring two goals each. The World Club Championship followed and also the European Super Cup. Marco was again voted European Footballer of the Year, in 1989.

The following season the Italians successfully defended their European Cup crown, beating Benefica 1-0 in the final in Vienna. The World Club Championship was retained and Van Basten topped the Italian scoring charts with 19 goals.

In a marvellous run of success, AC Milan won their first League title for four seasons in 1992. Van Basten contributed 25 goals from 31 matches and was Italy's leading scorer once more. He became only the third player to win the European Footballer of the Year award for a third time, Johan Cruyff and Michel Platini being the other two. He also won the World Player of the Year award for the second time as well as the newly-created FIFA World Footballer of the Year accolade. Then, to top it all, in December 1990 Marco scored five goals in an 8-0 win for Holland over Malta, equalling the Dutch record.

The 1992/93 season was his last as ankle injuries brought his career to an end. Mind you, he still managed to score 13 times in 15 games, and AC Milan won the Italian League yet again. Marco was only 28, a player still in his prime. It was a sad loss to the world game and, of course, a devastating blow for Van Basten. What a shock for a top player to wake up one morning with the realisation that his career was prematurely over. It calls for huge mental adjustment. You can imagine that at 28 years of age

ABOVE: **The joy of victory in the 1989 European Cup final in Barcelona.**

THE VENABLES VERDICT

- *Majestic Dutch striker with a real taste for goals.*

- *The foremost European centre-forward of the eighties and early nineties.*

- *In a fantastic club career, won the Dutch League title twice, the Italian League title three times, plus the European Cup in 1988/89 and 1989/90.*

- *Voted European Footballer of the Year three times, World Player of the Year twice, plus FIFA World Footballer of the Year.*

- *Ankle injuries forced a premature retirement, at the age of just 28.*

you're not thinking about retirement; you're concentrating only on playing in the next match and scoring the next goal.

For me the abiding memory of Marco Van Basten will be that beautiful goal he scored in the 1988 European Championship final against the USSR. It was a long cross from the left that he met with a fantastic, athletic volley from the narrowest of angles. The ball flew like an arrow into the far side of the net past a Soviet goalkeeper who was as surprised as the rest of us. It has to be one of the greatest goals ever scored in a major final.

BELOW: **Skilfully evading the firm challenge of Olympique Marseille's Basile Boli in the European Cup final of 1993.**

Tony Adams

A Born Leader

Tony Adams refused to be destroyed by his addiction to booze, the humiliation of being sent to prison and the other personal problems that would have finished a man weaker than himself.

I like Tony. I like his style. I admire anyone who can face up to adversity, admit they have to make changes, make these changes and come out on top. He was in all of my England teams and I am certain that all of us involved with the national side then now realise we would have been significantly weaker without him.

It's a pity our professional life together was so short as I would have liked to compete in a World Cup with him. It wasn't to be. I wasn't allowed the time to progress with England after Euro 96 and that's still one of these frustrations that nags away at

me from time to time. It's history now and I don't want to be accused of harping on about it but when I talk about Tony I realise that that England spell was so important, so engrossing for both of us.

Tony was the man I chose to take over as captain when David Platt was injured. David accepted the situation until he realised he had lost the job even when he was back and fit. Of course he lived with the fact but he wasn't happy about it. I just felt everything about Tony suggested leadership. He was a dominating player; the other players respected him. He knew how to cope with real difficulties. I suppose

> I just felt everything about Tony suggested leadership. He was a dominating player; the other players respected him.

you could say he accepted his own deficiencies and had worked hard to at least control them.

I also found him highly receptive to new ideas I had planned and wanted to first talk them through with him. I contacted him and arranged for us to have lunch at Scott's in Mount Street in London's West End. At that time I knew he was a heavy drinker; everyone, I think, would have known that. What I wasn't aware of was just how heavy, that he was an alcoholic, as he later publicly and bravely confessed. The irony was, as Tony explained in his autobiography *Addicted*, that the

LEFT: **Looking relaxed before a pre-season tournament in Amsterdam, August 2000.**

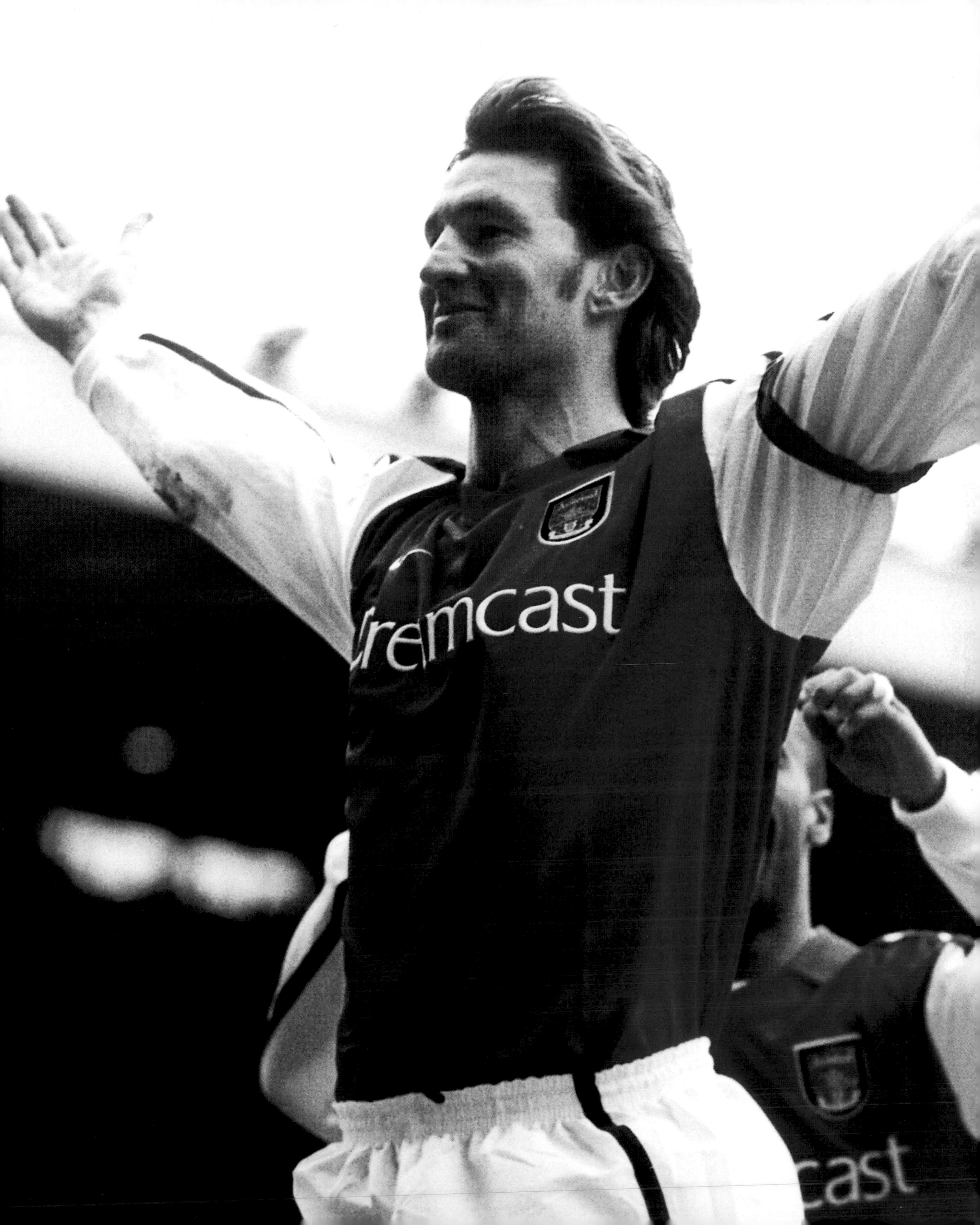
reamcast
cast

FACT FILE

FULL NAME: *Tony Alexander Adams*

BORN: *10 October 1966, Romford*

PLAYING CAREER
CLUBS: *Arsenal 1980-*

APPEARANCES/GOALS: *League 490(4)/32; FA Cup 50(1)/7; FL Cup 58(1)/5; European 48/3*

CAREER TOTAL: *646(6) appearances/47 goals*

HONOURS: *Premier League Champions 1997-98; Premier League runners-up 1998-99, 1999-2000, 2000-01; First Division Champions 1988-89, 1990-91; FA Cup Winners 1993, 1998 (Cup/League 'Double'); FA Cup Finalists 2000-01; League Cup Winners 1986-87, 1992-93; League Cup Finalists 1987-88; European Cup-Winners' Cup Winners 1993-94; European Cup-Winners' Cup Finalists 1994-95; UEFA Cup Finalists 1999-2000; PFA Young Player of the Year 1987*

INTERNATIONAL: *England 66 appearances/5 goals, 1987-2000*

Playing statistics complete to end of 2000-01 season

I went for seven attackers and just three defenders. What did Tony think, I wanted to know. It was important he was with me and I knew it would be difficult for him coming from his Arsenal background. Tony hadn't played this way before, but he was the starting point for it all.

He was cautious. He felt it was a bit too cavalier. We argued it out point by point. He asked questions, so I knew he was interested. In the end, we went for it and it took us to the semi-finals and unfortunately ultimate disappointment. But the sheer delight in beating Holland so comprehensively is a warm memory. I was very proud of Tony and the rest of the players on the night we did it. The atmosphere the players generated at Wembley made it an occasion that will live with me for ever.

Tony's nearing the end of his playing career and he has taken the first step by deciding, sensibly I think, that retiring from England duty will prolong the inevitable for just a little longer. The question

LEFT: **You won't find a more staunchly patriotic Englishman than Adams.**

glass or two of wine we had over lunch started him on one of his benders, for about six days if I remember correctly. If only I had known.

All I wanted from him on the day was to listen to what I had to say about my plans and then give his opinion on how we should approach our matches in the European Championship finals. I explained to him something along these lines: I wanted as many captains as I could muster. I started thinking in terms of attackers as in Bobby Charlton, and defenders as in his brother Jack. I thought, what would happen if we had five of each? Then I asked myself could we succeed with six attackers and four defenders. Then

He refused to be destroyed by his addiction to booze, the humiliation of being sent to prison and the other personal problems that would have finished a weaker man.

remains, what will he do when the moment comes?

Tony was always the first name on the team sheet because of his all-round ability and leadership qualities. Where Bobby Moore was a great captain who led by example in a quiet, dignified and calm manner, Tony was an 'up and at 'em type'. He was a very tough competitor and an intelligent player. He had a great way with players, even the more introverted

ones who wouldn't want to talk about their weaknesses; he sat and talked to them and drew them out. He was like the manager on the pitch, an outstanding right-hand man. I always wanted the players to understand my thinking and he was one of those who could transfer my philosophy and tactics to the players really well.

It would be simple to say that Tony will go into management, but it's never an easy transition. It's all about what he decides to do. Will it be management or coaching? Will he want to manage a big club straight away or take it step by step, building up to the big one? The same principles apply to coaching. Will he start from the bottom and work his way up surely and steadily

BELOW: **Organising England's defensive unit against Colombia at Wembley, September 1995.**

or dive straight in and quickly learn to swim?

You might think he would be ideally suited for either role but I am afraid it doesn't work that way. Of the players I have known over the years I would have bet on Frank McLintock, above all others, being an absolute certainty as a successful manager/coach. I can't be sure why it didn't work out for him, but it didn't. If Frank wasn't able to crack it coming from his background as an Arsenal captain, with his leadership style, then there are no guarantees for anyone. If you'd been forced to name the likeliest to succeed at management between Frank and George Graham, then most people who knew them would have gone for Frank – they would have been wrong. You ask yourself why, and factors like patience and tolerance come into the picture. I believe that what Tony has been through with his drink problem has made him more tolerant, forced him to slow down physically. It has also shown him he can be a winner if he focuses on any given role. I have no doubt that if

ABOVE: **Beating Manchester United's Jaap Stam and Peter Schmeichel in an aerial duel at Highbury, September 1998.**

Tony makes up his mind then he will be able to cope with the most formidable of tasks; that includes staying in the game beyond his playing career.

The day we were knocked out of Euro 96 was going to be my last day as England coach. I had known that for some time. My contract had been completed. It's never easy to accept defeat, never. They say going out in the semi-finals of any competition is worst of all. I accept that and have experienced the feeling, but losing on penalties to Germany once again in the semi-final of a European Championship tournament (second in status only to the World Cup) is particularly distressing. I had planned to speak to all the players as a group when

RIGHT: **Looking composed on the ball in an FA Cup tie in the middle of the 1998/99 season.**

we returned to our hotel but was so emotional I felt I would break down and be unable to finish what I wanted to say. In the end I spoke to each of them individually throughout the night, thanking them, remembering the good times and what had gone on during our time together. It was a very sad moment to say goodbye when we'd been together for so long and had worked so well as a team. It was very hard to say goodbye to Tony. I can't say enough about the work we put in together and what a great time it was for us.

Tony is one of Arsenal's all-time greats. The success of eight trophies won during the reigns of

> ## He accepted his own deficiencies and had worked hard to at least control them.

George Graham and Arsène Wenger has had one thing in common – Tony was there as the key player. He has pretty much won everything there is to win in modern football with the exception of the European Cup/Champions League. There could be no more fitting end than for him to be part of the Arsenal team that, hopefully, wins that trophy over the next two seasons. I'll continue watching his career with great interest.

THE VENABLES VERDICT

- *Unusual in the modern game – a one-club man. Has now clocked up 22 years at Highbury.*

- *An 'up and at 'em' type, a tough competitor, a hugely determined man.*

- *But also an intelligent player and an outstanding right-hand man for a manager.*

- *Well over 60 appearances for his country in a 13-year international career.*

- *Bravely confessed to alcohol addiction and has emerged a stronger individual.*

Teddy Sheringham

The Extraordinary Goalmaker

WHEN TEDDY SHERINGHAM CAME ON AS A LATE SUBSTITUTE FOR MANCHESTER UNITED IN WHAT WAS TO BE A STUNNING CLIMAX TO THE 1999 EUROPEAN CUP FINAL AGAINST BAYERN MUNICH, I WAS CERTAIN THE DECISION TO PLAY HIM WOULD TURN IT ROUND FOR UNITED.

I was right. I actually started laughing when Teddy scored United's equaliser, and I was still grinning when he laid on the winner for Ole Gunnar Solskjaer. It was sheer pleasure for me watching in the Camp Nou because everything I know about Teddy, everything I admire about him was encapsulated in those few minutes.

Let me explain. Teddy is a striver; everything he does, he does against the odds. He has never allowed himself the right to relax because any praise he receives has been so grudging. His pride stretches him to the great performances he has produced. It has always been that way for him, and it's the way he likes it. To some, United's position in those few remaining minutes was a lost cause, but Teddy

> **He has never allowed himself the right to relax because any praise he receives has been so grudging. His pride stretches him to the great performances he has produced.**

looked on it as an opportunity to defy the odds. He is not the type to be beaten psychologically – at least never in my experience. When a team is down and virtually out of such a major match the temptation is to pump the ball forward high in the hope that a

striker can get on to it. I knew Teddy would have none of that. He has the confidence, the belief in himself to do it his way, which for United on that night had to be to pass the ball. I knew he would demand that the players around him keep it on the deck to produce a goalscoring move. Win the ball, pass the ball, keep the ball moving, keep playing football, keep competing, never give in, never concede defeat. That is Teddy.

It was marvellous to watch that match unfold in the way it did. It was United's triumph, and Alex Ferguson's, but it was also a glorious victory for Teddy. I hope they don't begrudge me my satisfaction in watching a former player of mine achieve on the

THE VENABLES VERDICT

- *A top-flight goalscorer and a wonderful goalmaker.*

- *Great confidence and self-belief. Always competitive and determined.*

- *With Manchester United, has won the Champions League, the FA Cup and – three times – the Premier League title.*

- *Voted Footballer of the Year and PFA Player of the Year in 2001.*

- *Fast approaching 300 career goals in more than 650 appearances in professional football.*

biggest club stage what I knew he was capable of and others said he wasn't.

Teddy started out as one half of a highly successful partnership with Tony Cascarino at Millwall. They were much sought after as a result. The main target was Cascarino, but I always leaned towards Teddy's ability; he was the one I knew I would take should I ever have the chance. I think others were put off Teddy because he was slower than Cascarino. I didn't see that as a handicap. In fact, when you analyse these matters it is often those with a weakness who recognise the flaw and work hard to counter it. You must have the attitude which compels you to listen, to learn and to react. Teddy did that. He developed a game which not only presents him with the opportunity to score but has made those he partners, the players who have worked alongside him like Alan Shearer, Jurgen Klinsmann, Andy Cole, Nick Barmby and Tony Cascarino, very happy men indeed. When he is playing they are virtually guar-

> It was sheer pleasure for me watching in the Camp Nou because everything I know about Teddy, everything I admire about him was encapsulated in those few minutes.

anteed goals. I'm not saying the likes of Shearer or Klinsmann wouldn't have scored without Teddy – of course they would. He just makes it easier for them, even when, as with Cole, he doesn't talk to the man on or off the field.

I have always thought that when Aston Villa signed Cascarino they signed the wrong player – and I don't mean that to sound in any way disrespectful to a very competent player who represented the Republic of Ireland with great distinction on many occasions. It simply reflects my belief that Teddy has more to offer a team as a football player.

At the back of my mind too, as I watched those final minutes in Barcelona, was the thought that this was the perfect answer to those irate England supporters who used to write letters criticising me for selecting Teddy when I was national coach. Some of those letters were shocking, the gist of all but a few, 'Why do you keep selecting your friend? I don't understand why you think he's a top player.' My reply to that was, 'You're right. You don't understand.' They should have learned the answers to their questions from his performances in Euro 96. If not, hopefully it sank in after that wonderful European Cup final.

Teddy gave out confusing signals about his physical strength, and that was another asset of his. Those who didn't know saw him as a soft touch when he was anything but. For a player of his high skill level he could never be kicked out of a game – and plenty have tried over the years. We have seen, for instance, Glenn Hoddle's impact on a match considerably reduced by certain types of tackling, but Teddy is more

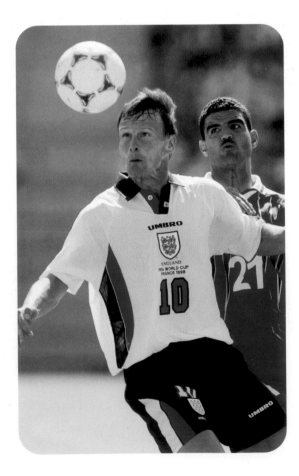

LEFT: **Keeping the Tunisians at bay during the 1998 World Cup finals.**

like Paul Gascoigne in this respect: he is a player of exquisite skill and there is no way you can kick him out of his stride.

Teddy is a top-flight goalscorer and an extraordinary goalmaker. He can score from anywhere and make them from anywhere. Under me, his attitude was faultless. He gave everything, was serious about the game, listened to what was said and took on board what he felt was useful to his game.

ABOVE: **Teddy celebrates his last-gasp equalising goal in 1999's Champions League final.**

It surprised me when he decided to return to Tottenham and join former England coach Glenn Hoddle. I don't think Glenn treated him as well as he should have done prior to the 1998 World Cup in France when Teddy was involved in some trouble in Portugal after the squad had been allowed a short break. Glenn should have either dropped him then or kept him and protected him. He kept him and played him, but I didn't think Teddy would forgive or forget. He has, though, and that's a good thing. Spurs now have a player some will be saying is too old, well past his best. Teddy will love that.

FACT FILE

FULL NAME: *Edward Paul Sheringham*

BORN: *2 April 1966, Highams Park, Walthamstow*

PLAYING CAREER

CLUBS: *Millwall 1984–91; Aldershot (on loan) 1985; Nottingham Forest 1991–92; Tottenham Hotspur 1992–97 and 2001– ; Manchester United 1997–2001*

APPEARANCES/GOALS:

	League	FA Cup	FL Cup	European
Millwall	205(15)/93	12/5	16(1)/8	
Aldershot	4(1)/0			
Nottm Forest	42/14	4/2	10/5	
Tottenham	163(3)/76	17/13	14/10	
Man Utd	73(31)/31	4(5)/5	1/1	20(11)/9

CAREER TOTAL: *585(67) appearances/272 goals*

HONOURS: *Premier League Champions 1998–99, 1999–2000, 2000–01; FA Cup Winners 1998–99; UEFA Champions League Winners 1998–99; Inter Continental Cup Winners 1999; Footballer of the Year 2001; PFA Player of the Year 2001 (all with Manchester United); Second Division Champions 1987–88 (with Millwall)*

INTERNATIONAL: *England 39 appearances/9 goals, 1993–2000 Playing statistics complete to end of 2000–01 season*

Paul Gascoigne

Unpredictable Genius

Without doubt, Paul Gascoigne was one of the most gifted footballers of his generation, an attacking midfielder of great imagination, ingenuity and flair, possessing a shrewd football brain, a delightful touch, a subtle pass and great awareness of what is going on around him.

Indeed, Gazza would have been considered uniquely talented in any era - his special flair on the pitch, not just on the training pitch, was incredible. He had this strength too, a physical strength which meant you weren't going to be able to kick him out of the game. He was also a giver. The players loved him and he would always do you a favour rather than do you any harm. Sometimes he went too far when it came to taking the mickey, but if he saw he'd gone too far

he would apologise immediately in front of everyone. And to cap it all, he was brilliant with the youngsters. After training at Tottenham he would join the youth team for about fifteen minutes and work with them.

I think there is one occasion which sums up the loyalty he inspired. He was due to go to Lazio but his fitness was in question and it was decided that the Italians would come over and we would have a game laid on so they could watch him. It was the close sea-

> I'd leave him alone to get on with playing football and I was tolerant of him, but if he stepped out of place he knew he'd get pulled up and told to toe the line.

son and all the other clubs had finished, so we asked the youth team to come in and play. There was no pressure, they didn't have to do it, but they all turned up. Paul gave them all £50 and insisted they took it even though they didn't want to. He wasn't showing off, he was just a giver. That was the way he was.

I have a lot of good things to say about Gazza and about his past footballing highs, but what worries me is his future. He has all the qualities to be a good coach. He has the information, he's warm, he plays the game with great feeling and he'd put the time in,

LEFT: **Playing for his hometown club, Newcastle United, April 1988.**

FACT FILE

FULL NAME: *Paul John Gascoigne*

BORN: *27 May 1967, Gateshead*

PLAYING CAREER
CLUBS: *Newcastle United 1984–88; Tottenham Hotspur 1988–92; Lazio (Italy) 1992–95; Rangers 1995–98; Middlesbrough 1998–2000; Everton 2000–*

APPEARANCES/GOALS:

	League	FA Cup	FL Cup	European
Newcastle United	83(9)/21	4/3	8/1	2(1)/0
Tottenham Hotspur	91(1)/19	6/6	14(1)/8	
Lazio	41/6			
Rangers	74/30	7(1)/3	7/4	16/2
Middlesbrough	39(3)/4	2/0	3(2)/0	
Everton	10(4)/0		0(1)/0	

CAREER TOTAL: *407(23) appearances/107 goals*

HONOURS: *FA Cup Winners 1991 (with Tottenham Hotspur); Scottish League Champions 1995–96, 1996–97; Scottish Cup Winners 1996; Scottish League Cup Winners 1996–97; Scottish Footballer of the Year 1995–96; Scottish PFA Player of Year 1995-96 (all with Rangers)*

INTERNATIONAL: *England 57 appearances/10 goals, 1989–98*

HONOURS: *World Cup Semi-final 1990; European Championship Semi-final 1996*

Playing statistics complete to end of 2000-01 season

but he needs to be consistently serious about something. Having said that, the biggest shock I ever had with Gazza was hearing about his attitude when angling. When he was with England he and David Seaman would go fishing, and Gazza wouldn't tolerate anyone messing about. He demanded complete peace and quiet. He wouldn't let Paul Stewart go with him as he was always talking and larking around, but to Gazza fishing was a serious business. He was a completely different person on the riverbank. Maybe if he could translate that calmness to the pitch then he could be a success as a coach. It just goes to show that when he's passionate about something he can be deadly serious and give it one hundred per cent concentration and effort.

ABOVE RIGHT: **Another goal for Spurs, and another confident celebration routine.**

You never quite knew where you were with Paul, and it was that unpredictability that made him the great player he was. He could turn a game around himself. I've seen him gather up the rest of the team, push them along and win a game virtually single-handedly. He also loves football, which is an important point. He would be first in for training and last away. He was never happier than when he had a ball at his feet. When he was a kid growing up in Gateshead, the neighbours would know when Gazza was around as they'd hear the thump, thump of the football as he kicked it against their front doors and played in the street with the other boys.

But opposing this sublime talent he had a self-destruct button which he was never far away from pushing. He led a chaotic private life, which was often played out in public, and he was basically insecure and shy even though he covered that up with his outrageous exploits and jokes. Nevertheless, I enjoyed having him in my team, and I think that maybe I was the coach who got the best out of him. I'd leave him alone to get on with playing football and I was tolerant of him, but if he stepped out of place he knew he'd get pulled up and told to toe the line. As a coach, you can't let one player get away with too much as it would unsettle the team, the others thinking he was getting preferential treatment

> **Gazza was a completely different person on the riverbank. Maybe if he could translate that calmness to the pitch then he could be a success as a coach.**

and not pulling his weight. The strange thing was that with Gazza you never had to worry about him pulling his weight. He was so keen on football that he wouldn't let you down on the pitch however bad things were off it.

This sense of extreme commitment was nowhere more on display than in Turin in 1990. For that World Cup Bobby Robson had adopted a sweeper system which gave Paul the midfield support necessary to carry out his playmaking duties. The tears flowed during the semi-final when he was booked, the caution meaning that he would miss the final should England get through. Those television pictures made him famous throughout England and the world. His loyalty and patriotism were such that he couldn't imagine missing the final. In the end, of course, he did miss it – along with the rest of the players in the England squad.

Gazza first became famous with the Toon Army at Newcastle, who saw something of themselves in Gascoigne. Paul had made over a hundred first-team appearances there, not to mention his eighteen games at England Under-21 level, when Tottenham came in with a £2 million bid for him. As Newcastle

BELOW: **Giving a group of photographers an image to remember during England's World Cup quarter-final against Cameroon, July 1990.**

were not a wealthy club at this stage, the offer was accepted. I was at White Hart Lane fresh from Barcelona and we set off into a new era together. Spurs fans have always appreciated flair and skill.

Gary Lineker was also in that team, but he and Gazza were like chalk and cheese in terms of personality. They rarely mixed socially, but there is one story about them that I like. They had gone to dinner, and as they came out of the restaurant Gazza said, 'Let's go to a nightclub.' Gary was not a nightclub type, but to help make the new Spurs recruit feel at home he agreed, and they went off to find a taxi. After ten minutes or so there were still no free taxis so Gary suggested they give up on the nightclub, but Gazza was having none of it. A bus passed, and he pulled Gary on board. The passengers couldn't believe it when these two high-profile footballers got on. Gazza, in his inimitable way, said, 'Take us to the nearest club, please!' Surprisingly the bus driver agreed, and they all lurched off into the night taking a new and different route. Gazza stood at the front conducting the whole bus in a rendition of 'We're all going on a summer holiday'. He was like that; he could brighten up people's lives with his sense of humour and desire to entertain and please.

On the pitch, his highly extrovert personality was always in evidence. In 1991, we met Arsenal at Wembley in the FA Cup semi-final, the Gunners supposedly on for the Double before Gazza put us on the road to the final with a sensational swerving free-kick from 35 yards.

However, in the final itself came the downside of Gascoigne. He was completely hyped up and out of control. He charged around the pitch making wild tackles before lunging at Nottingham Forest's wing-back, Gary Charles, just outside the area. Charles was injured and Gascoigne damaged his cruciate ligaments, putting his transfer to Italian club Lazio in jeopardy. Gazza's injuries were almost always caused by him going to ground in a challenge. I must have warned him a hundred times to stay on his feet, that if he did that

LEFT: **Frightening Italian defences during his spell in Serie A with Lazio in August 1993.**

RIGHT: **Relishing the physical challenge of an Old Firm derby in January 1997.**

he wouldn't get injured. Lazio were very patient and waited until 1992 for him. He went on to have a successful time in Rome, although he was also dogged by controversy.

After Italy Gascoigne headed to Scotland and Rangers. He hit controversy there as well when, after scoring a goal, he celebrated by mimicking a fife player, actions which are associated with Protestant marches. Glasgow is a highly sectarian city so this didn't go down too well with the Catholic Celtic supporters. Despite this *faux pas*, Paul enjoyed great personal success with Rangers with two successive League Championships, the Scottish Cup in 1996 and the League Cup in 1997. He was also voted Footballer of the Year by the Scottish writers and PFA Player of the Year by his fellow professionals. His goal ratio of 30 in 74 matches was the best of his career. He then went on to Middlesbrough, and from there to Goodison Park to play for ex-Rangers manager Walter Smith.

I have many good memories of Paul Gascoigne. We had a great relationship. He played some of his best football at Spurs under me, and of course during Euro 96 when I was England manager. I will always remember his goal against Scotland in that tournament, which to my mind was one of the best goals ever scored at Wembley and one which will go down in the history books. I'll never forget his 'nearly' goal either – remember? The one against Germany in extra time at Wembley during Euro 96? I still have nightmares about him not knocking that one in.

I sincerely hope that whatever the future holds for him he'll find inner peace and strength and never lose his sense of fun and his ability to brighten all our lives with his well-developed capacity for really enjoying his football.

Alan Shearer

The Even-keeled Marksman

THERE HAVE BEEN LOTS OF OCCASIONS WHEN I JUST COULDN'T UNDERSTAND THE PUBLIC'S ATTITUDE TO CERTAIN PLAYERS. PEOPLE WOULD SAY TO ME, 'THAT SHEARER'S A BIT OF A COLD FISH' AND I'D SAY, 'NO, HE'S ONE OF THE JOKERS IN THE SQUAD'.

There are very few 'names', if we can call them that, who actually represent themselves in public exactly as they are in private or as a footballer with the rest of the players. When you are close to the scene it really is difficult to comprehend why some players are so highly regarded and some become such easy targets for criticism. It is only when you stand back, even a little, that you begin to appreciate what the outsider means.

Alan doesn't come over cold or diffident so much as serious. When you see him on television you could think maybe there isn't a lot of fun inside him, that he must be as ruthlessly committed off the field as he is on it. In reality he has a terrific sense of humour and is something of a mischievous practical joker (but never anything nasty). The game's not about 'having an image' so far as Alan is concerned. What you see is Alan Shearer, but it's Shearer the pro-

> **When they talk about England's all-time great centre-forwards then the name Alan Shearer will always sit comfortably alongside the Lawtons and the Lofthouses.**

fessional, not the one those close to him recognise. He knows how to relax, and, most importantly, when to relax. But of course he is single-minded when it comes to his profession, and he will put everything into achieving his ambitions. He worked for me with England and the 'serious' side of his character was

what we needed on the field. We also needed his self-belief when the hounds were snapping round his heels, when it would have been easier for him to walk away without playing in Euro 96.

I've been a Shearer admirer since I first heard his name and went out of my way to watch him play, in his very early days at Southampton – before he had actually made his senior debut.

I was told then that he was going to develop into a supreme goalscorer, though the

BELOW: **Another determined surge towards goal for Blackburn Rovers, April 1995.**

chances of my working with him were remote – unless I became England coach. When I did take over at national level he was the striker I knew I could rely on, through good spells and bad – and remember, every goalscorer has periods when nothing seems to go right. That was exactly the situation facing Alan before Euro 96. Had I listened to some of the critics I would have discarded him and the European Championship would have had to look elsewhere for its top scorer.

England has been extremely fortunate in terms of strikers, at no other time than when Alan Shearer was there, ready to step into the breach as soon as Gary Lineker stood down and retired. On their day they were equally devastating; I don't think it is necessary to try to divide them and assess their relative importance to England in recent years. Alan perfected the art of scoring

BELOW RIGHT: **Who will ever forget the defeat of Holland at Euro 96? Alan comes in for some close attention from Winston Bogarde during that game.**

from any given position. He scored short or long, from a six-yard touch to a 30-yard thunderbolt. He could use his left foot, his right foot or his head. He could work the near post or the far post. He could play wide and did so to great effect to allow others a way through. When it came to scoring, nothing seemed impossible. And there were those who wanted me to drop him from the Euro 96 squad.

I accept he went into a bit of a trough prior to the finals, but not only did I never think of dropping him I never asked him to explain why he hadn't been scoring. The only thing he said to me, regularly as it happens, was that he couldn't wait for the opening match, and in my experience when players say that you are in business. I knew, he knew, that come the day he would produce the goods – and he did. His partnership with Teddy Sheringham was a dream one for England.

Alan has cost two record transfers: Southampton sold him to Blackburn Rovers for £3.6 million the year the Premier League was launched, then in July 1996 he went from Rovers to Newcastle for £15 million. He survived cruciate ligament damage in his first season with the Lancashire club, recovering to help Rovers finish behind Manchester United the next season with the man himself scoring 31 goals. Indeed, he finished as the Premier League's top

FACT FILE

FULL NAME: *Alan Shearer OBE*

BORN: *13 August 1970, Newcastle-upon-Tyne*

PLAYING CAREER

CLUBS: *Southampton 1988–92; Blackburn Rovers 1992–96; Newcastle United 1996–*

APPEARANCES/GOALS:

	League	FA Cup	FL Cup	European
Southampton	*105(13)/23*	*11(3)/4*	*16(2)/11*	
Blackburn Rovers	*132(6)/112*	*8/2*	*16/14*	*9/2*
Newcastle United	*130(4)/69*	*21/16*	*8/4*	*13/4*

CAREER TOTAL: *469(28) appearances/261 goals*

HONOURS: *Premier League Champions 1994–95 (with Blackburn Rovers); Premier League runners-up 1993–94 (with Blackburn Rovers), 1996–97 (with Newcastle United); FA Cup Finalists 1997–98, 1998–99 (with Newcastle United); Footballer of the Year 1994; PFA Player of the Year 1995, 1997; awarded the OBE, 2001*

INTERNATIONAL: *England 63 appearances/30 goals, 1992–2000; England U-21 11 appearances/13 goals, 1991–92*

Playing statistics complete to end of 2000–01 season

The game's not about 'having an image' so far as Alan is concerned. What you see is Alan Shearer, but it's Shearer the professional, not the one those close to him recognise.

ABOVE: **Yet another goal for Alan, this time in the black and white of his beloved Newcastle United, September 1999.**

striker in three successive seasons with 34, 31 and 25 goals – oh, and he helped the club bank-rolled by the late Jack Walker to the championship in 1995.

At the time of my writing this book there are concerns about his fitness and a recommendation from all those who care about him that he should get plenty of rest and take the long route back. I suspect he hasn't.

The only time he has really surprised me was when he decided to call it a day with England. I say surprised, but in fact the reasons he gave were perfectly understandable: he wanted to spend more time

with his family, his body wasn't getting any younger, something had to be sacrificed and it couldn't be his club career at Newcastle. So his international career is at an end, but when they talk about England's all-time great centre-forwards then the name Alan Shearer will always sit comfortably alongside the Lawtons and the Lofthouses.

Acknowledgements

I would like to thank Jane Nottage and Alex Montgomery for assisting me in writing this book. And thanks to my wife for the funny bits in the book and for taking all the pictures! Finally, a mention for my number one hero, Boo the golden Labrador, whose bravery in saving Toby the golden retriever from drowning was astounding. *Terry Venables*

Like a great many books, this one started off as a gem of an idea which developed over a very pleasant, long lunch at a London watering hole. The host was Jonathan Taylor, football fan and Virgin Books' sports publisher. Jonathan had just published *Murray Walker's Formula One Heroes*, which was proving to be highly successful; he thought a similar book on football would be exciting and interesting. It took about five seconds to decide who should write it – there was only one name and that was Terry Venables. At the time Terry was working for ITV and I was resting between books. Since then Terry has saved Middlesbrough from the ignominy of relegation and I have followed Murray and been sucked into the high-octane, fast-moving world of F1 as Diary Editor of *Formula One Magazine*.

But in between football matches and F1 races, when Terry and I managed to sit down in one place, the book took shape and the Heroes came alive. Some of the names are very personal to Terry and from his past, some are well known, and some are friends and colleagues from the game.

As we chatted about the men and, of course, women – his wife and daughters – who have shaped his life, it got me thinking about my own heroes. Who would they be? Undoubtedly, joint number ones would be my parents, who have given me the love and support necessary for success in the insecure world of writing. But also high on my list would be Terry. He and his wife, Toots, have become close friends of mine over the last ten years or so. We have seen each other through good and bad times, success and failure, happiness and disaster. Funnily enough it's disaster that forms the character and builds the bonds. That much-missed, generous, and warm-hearted best friend of Terry's Bobby Keetch used to say that what doesn't destroy you will make you stronger. How true. If you can face disaster and difficulties full in the face and cope, then you'll come out stronger and wiser. But it takes a very special person to face disaster in the public arena; Terry has not only faced it but emerged the victor.

I can't think of anything worse than facing total ruin and having people you've never met making daily comment on it. It would be easy to become cynical and bitter, and I'm sure the accusations have hurt at times, but the great thing about Terry is that after all his problems in the past, he is still the same bouncy, optimistic chappy, with the happy smile who brightens up your life with a joke and a laugh. Believe me, smiling when your world is collapsing is not easy, and Terry is my hero because he has been through the bad times and come through smiling. When I have to face challenges in my life, Terry is the inspiration that I look to. If he can deal with anything that life throws at him, then so can I, and he has often unknowingly helped me to deal with problems. I am sure he has helped many people he has never even met to face life with a smile.

Equally heroic is his wife, Toots, who is a loyal and intelligent adviser not only to her husband but also to her friends. Of course, there are many people who are heroes not because they have achieved fame and fortune, but because they have brought happiness to others in difficult circumstances. The people who manage to smile through life's storms are my heroes and Terry, along with my parents, Geoffrey and Margaret, are top of my list.

Jane Nottage

The publishers would like to thank:

Jen Little and everyone at Empics Sports Photo Agency for their painstaking picture research; Jo Hill and Simon Balley at Balley Design Associates; John Fennelly and Jon Rayner of Tottenham Hotspur FC for permission to quote from the official matchday programme's obituary of Danny Blanchflower; John Russell for providing all the statistical information. In turn, John would like to thank Tony Matthews (Aberdeen FC), Andy Porter (Heart of Midlothian FC), Dave Copping (Hibernian FC), David Downes (Glentoran FC), Graham Haynes (PFA), Ian Rigby (Waterlooville Public Library), Graham Newnham, Philip Stephenson, Roy France, Martijn Wassen (KNVB) and Emma Biggs for their assistance. The following sources were used during the research process: *The PFA Players' Records 1946–1998* by Barry J Hugman (Queen Anne Press); *Premier League Record File* by Bruce Smith (Virgin Books); *The Complete Encyclopedia of Football* by Keir Radnedge (Carlton Books); *The Sunday Times Illustrated History of Football* by Chris Nawrat and Steve Hutchings (Hamlyn); *English Football – A Fan's Handbook* by Dan Golstein (Penguin Books); *The United Alphabet* by Garth Dykes (ACL & Polar Publishing); *100 Seasons of League Football* by Bryon Butler (Queen Anne Press); *The Official Illustrated History of the FA Cup* by Bryon Butler (Queen Anne Press); *Rothman's Football Yearbook* (various) by Glenda and Jack Rollin (Headline); *Arsenal Fact File* by Bruce Smith and John Russell (Virgin Books).

Picture credits

Empics Sports Photo Agency: pages 4/5, 12/13, 22/23, 30, 32, 35 (*both*), 43, 46, 47, 48, 50/51, 55, 57, 58, 59, 64, 79, 84, 87, 88, 90 (*top*), 93, 94, 95, 97, 98, 100, 109, 116, 117, 118, 119, 122, 129, 135, 136, 137, 139, 140, 148, 158, 159, 160, 164, 167, 168, 174, 177, 178, 179, 181, 183, 184, 185, 186 and 190/191. **Allsport (UK) Ltd:** pages 17, 96, 99, 101, 105, 108, 111, 120, 121, 125, 138, 142, 144, 145, 147, 149, 156, 162, 163, 165, 169, 170, 171, 172, 173, 175, 182 and 187. **Hulton Getty:** pages 16, 19, 27, 28, 29, 33, 37, 38, 40, 42, 44, 45, 53, 65, 67, 75, 76, 77, 83, 91, 114 and 127. **Popperfoto:** pages 31, 36, 39, 41, 52, 54, 62, 63, 66, 68, 69, 71, 78, 80, 81, 82, 85, 86, 89 (*both*), 90 (*bottom*), 102, 103, 104, 106, 107, 110, 112, 113, 115, 123, 124, 126, 128, 130/131, 133, 134, 141, 143, 146, 151, 157, 161, 166, 180, 188 and 189. **Action Images:** pages 73, 153, 154 and 155. **Colorsport:** page 24. **Topham Picturepoint:** pages 60 and 61. **Terry Venables:** pages 9, 10, 15 and 192. **Ken Jones:** pages 20 and 21.